\ I /

# 25 Brilliant Business Mentors
*Their Top Tips to Catapult You to Success*

## Also by Splendor Publishing

*The Art & Science of Loving Yourself First*
*'cause your business should complete you, not deplete you!*

*Speak and Grow Niche*

*The Reframing Book*

*Discover Your Brilliance*

*Out-of-the-Box Marketing & Promotion*

*Accessorizing for Design Professionals*

*Color for Design Professionals*

*Moneytudes*

\ I /

# 25 Brilliant Business Mentors
*Their Top Tips to Catapult You to Success!*

## Co-authored by

Tim G. Carter, Jasmin Christensen,
Rick Cooper, Margo DeGange, Barbara Drohan Dooley,
Patty Farmer, Carla Ferrer, Steve Gutzler, Leslie Hassler,
Julie M. Holloway, Marybeth Hrim, Ann Jenrette-Thomas,
Lisa Mohl Kaplin, Kathi C. Laughman, Blaze Lazarony,
Diana Matteson-Oliveira, Kat Mikic, Kimberly Pitts,
Lisa Rehurek, Tracy Repchuk, Carrie Sharpshair,
Shari Strong, Ha Tran, Liz Uram, Alicia White

## Compiled by

Margo DeGange, M.Ed.

Splendor Publishing
College Station, TX

SPLENDOR PUBLISHING
Published by Splendor Publishing
College Station, TX.

First published printing, November 2013

Library of Congress Control Number: 2013919726
25 Brilliant Business Mentors
Their Top Tips to Catapult You to Success
1. Business 2. Marketing

ISBN-10:1940278023
ISBN-13:978-1-940278-02-5

Business/Marketing
Printed in the United States of America.

Artwork: Glopphy 933690 | Vectorstock
Cover layout: JMH Creative Solutions

For more information, or to order bulk copies of this book for events, seminars, conferences, or training, please contact SplendorPublishing.com.

## Dedication

This book is dedicated to the motivated and enlightened entrepreneurs who are determined to succeed brilliantly in business, and to the inspired individuals with important and meaningful life-work, who help others live better lives. You have the will, you have the desire, you have the reason. Now we give you knowledge that will make all the difference!

# ≷Contents≶

# ⊱Introduction⊰

Have you ever wished you could ask a noted and successful expert a very specific question relating to the areas that affect your business the most? Wouldn't it be phenomenal if those answers were right at your fingertips, without having to sort through countless "fluffy" articles, or pages and pages of online search results (only to come away as stumped as you were before, and a lot more exhausted)?

So often, business owners just need some to-the-point, tried and proven advice from those who've gone before, so they can get on with the business of doing business and making profits.

In this quick-reference book for small business owners and business-builders, 25 of the most brilliant business mentors come together to share their top business tips, strategies, and tactics, to make it easy for you to succeed as an entrepreneur!

These magical pages cover everything from right thinking and believing, to powerful productivity, and leading your business for success. They uncover some of the very best and most effective marketing tools and activities you can use and do, to gain great exposure and attract your very best clients.

Need help with your sales process? Is closing the sale a challenge for you? Are you stumped on strategy? No more! Increasing sales and profits got easier the second you picked up this book! Gain wisdom on pricing your products and services, and investing in your business. Uncover the money secrets that elevate entrepreneurs to the top of their dreams!

Each author has been challenged to respond to five significant business prompts in five key areas, including:

1

1. Mindset
2. Business Management (running a business)
3. Visibility (marketing)
4. Sales
5. Money

The **Mindset Tips** address your thoughts. They will help you to create a better life and business through empowered thinking, visualizing, and believing.

The **Business Management Tips** relate to the day-to-day operations of running and managing a business. They include productivity, systems, your team, resources, measurement, environment, leadership, tools, and the things that will help you run your business more smoothly and brilliantly.

The **Visibility Tips** are all about marketing, with specific actions you can take to gain exposure and attract clients. Many of these ideas address the "why" or the "how," and come from the assumption that you already have a good idea of who *your* ideal clients are. Here, our experts focus on giving you tips, top secrets, and golden nuggets for gaining greater visibility.

The **Sales Tips** cover just about every aspect of selling, with tips relating to the sales process, closing the sale, scripts, strategy calls, triggering interest, and much more ingenious input, all directly related to increasing sales to increase profits.

The **Money Tips** are thoughts, ideas, and suggestions the authors strongly believe will help you—the entrepreneur—to prosper financially. These cover everything from how to make it, keep it, think about it, and invest it, to establishing powerful money goals for growth, and creating wealth and prosperity.

This book is a business work of art, designed with one clear goal: to move you forward quickly in your business, so you can thrive, excel, and enjoy greater profits. Each page is full of wisdom, know-how, and real-life business experience, to help you gain insight and direction for wild business success, with proven action-steps to make it exciting and possible!

The authors know how to mentor you. They've created lives for themselves that many people dream of living. Their sales records, balanced approach, and happiness scores speak for themselves. Some of them are a tad bit intellectual and formal; others are "meat and potatoes" casual; but *all* offer caring intentions and "rubber meets the road" advice you can relate to.

As I ponder the five categories of business support that make up the heart of this work, I see them each as absolutely crucial. From my work helping clients to gain visibility, I know that business success is not *just* about marketing.

It begins with a solid product or service you feel compelled to bring to the marketplace, but that's not enough! You can't market effectively without a mindset of confidence in yourself, your purpose, and your offerings. Even with confidence and top-shelf products or services, you can't be efficient or run your business properly without good management. Still, even with all of *that*, no one would benefit from your offers unless you clearly communicated the right message, through the right channels, to the right people, so they'd want a conversation with you. *Then*, when you sat with them to chat, you'd have to know how to convert their needs, desires, and enthusiasm into cash. Finally, even with cash in hand, it would do you no good if you didn't value, respect, and wisely invest your money.

5 key business prompts. 125 powerful responses. If you know you're ready to prosper, but need help getting there, let the 25 brilliant business mentors in this book help catapult you to success!

To Your Brilliance,

*Margo DeGange*

# Chapter 1

# ≥Brilliant Tips≤ from Tim G. Carter

## Tim G. Carter's Top Mindset Tip

Powerful Concepts are more easily absorbed and utilized, when represented by something we can remember. Hope and incurable optimism are the driving forces behind every entrepreneur. We believe we can achieve, or we would never try. So the easy memory word for your victory mindset is *hope*.

Consider this definition of *hope* to empower your new business ideas. H.O.P.E. equals High Octane Positive Energy. The fuel propelling you to action will either sustain you through the growth of your business, or cause you to give up when the chips are down.

So here are some specific ideas on how to integrate and harness High Octane Positive Energy in your business mindset.

1. Resolve to have guts. You can't score a home run until you swing. And when you swing, you must hit it squarely and follow through fully.

2. Harness the power of multiplied results. Use this power phrase: *Positive x Positive = Unlimited*! To win, you must form a chain of good reinforcing behaviors. Then, consistently apply these actions. This focus will lead to the addition and multiplication of your efforts.

3.  Work on a healthy sense of worth. Find, accept, and practice your own value. Self-worth is not selfish. Value cannot be given, unless possessed first. You must own it before you can give it away.

4.  Invest yourself in your goals. Harness the power of resolve. Be committed to your work.

5.  Learn to look at things from different perspectives. Look at your challenges upside down and inside out. Take another point of view, often.

6.  Know your "why." No venture can be sustained without a good reason. Motivation only works, when for a purpose.

7.  Fulfill your potential. Start now and stay on task. Utilize inventive determination. Practice *creating* solutions.

Follow these concepts to invest High Octane Positive Energy in your business.

## Tim G. Carter's Top Business Management Tip

Going into a business is in many respects, like going into a marriage. It is wise to plan in advance; for counselors to help you, if you have problems! Have a proactive plan for overcoming challenges and growing. Problems are normal in everything, especially in business. To increase your odds of success, anticipate roadblocks.

Difficulties will happen. Problems will occur. Decide up front, how to get the advice of others already successful in the field you're going into. Begin networking with great minds of those with a strong track record in your field. There is no time more difficult to gain inspiration—and yet more critical to do so—than when you are in the midst of the problems of a growing business.

Adopt an accountability partner with a winning professional record. I have found it critical in past endeavors and necessary for future business plans, to follow examples of successful models. This is important for creating a business, as well as for growing it. Your success scenario greatly improves when you have good advisers.

Accountability keeps you on track. Good business allies will hold you to your word. They will tell you the truth, when others won't. Link up now with wise advisers. There are mentors in nearly every field who will help you evaluate and improve, if you let them.

Pride goes before a fall. Don't be afraid to ask how to best manage your business operations. The wiser I become with God's help, the more I need the advice of others. We often cannot see things about ourselves that we really need to see.

Ask qualified leaders for advice about your business practices, and be prepared to appreciate what they say—even when you don't like it! Be proactive now. Plan to have wise business advisers.

## Tim G. Carter's Top Visibility Tip

### *Create an Effective Business Referral Program*

No business succeeds to its highest potential without maximizing assets. One asset that should be developed in nearly every business context is the revenue generating practice of referrals.

A referral program acquires customers from existing customers or prospects. It is a quick way to jump-start your business, without a whole lot of expense. You can create a dynamic referral program based on your own passionate sense of mission.

How? Let each communication with a prospect not only build your business with them, but also cause them to help build your business with their friends or contacts. Encourage them to help their friends. Make it worth their time to sell others on the awesome mission and benefits of your product or service.

Sometimes a cash or prize incentive can really get this ball rolling. This marketing strategy utilizes synergy (multiple benefits to each action). Also, it is a natural sales growth tool with nearly unlimited applications. Some version will work in almost every selling environment.

Build your referral program into the practice script of every stage of your sales process, from first meeting to final closing. (This is important. Make a plan for how you will build referrals into the fabric of your sales environment, and evaluate every month or so.) At least 30 percent of sales in my current selling arena are generated by this technique.

Not only can you promote new clients through existing ones, but there are also ways to encourage your business networking colleagues to be your promoters.

The Power of duplication works in any endeavor. Here are some reasons why you should incorporate referral selling into your enterprise:

> Defrays advertising costs
> Maximizes inspiring, cooperative efforts
> Builds brand name recognition
> Creates healthy buying conditions

> ≩ Pre-answers objections of prospects
> ≩ Provides a wealth of testimonials, endorsements, and proof sources

**Tim G. Carter's Top Sales Tip**

In a past interview process, there were hundreds of applicants. The field narrowed to five industry sales leaders, including myself. After the first day of intense interviews, I knew meeting the president the next day would make it or break it.

At a bar in Atlanta (I no longer drink), I ordered a Guinness and was fascinated with the ping-pong like ball that made it pour like an actual draft beer. I tore the can apart and investigated. I had my answer about how to stand out with the company president.

Walking in, I noticed his desk stacked with resumes. As we talked, I played with something in my fingers (making sure he noticed). At a certain point, I literally rolled the ball under my hand. He knew I was up to something and with a wry grin said, "OK, you've succeeded. Why do you play with a ping-pong ball during our interview?"

With a grin, equal to his, I explained how the ball belonged in a Guinness can, and how it worked to increase value and sales appeal. I asked him to imagine profits, realized by the company, because of the individual who thought up the idea.

The point? If he procured my services, I would do that for his company, namely, find never before imagined applications, markets, and profits for his product.

So, I urged him to consider the ping-pong ball's originality in the Guinness can, especially when thinking about my potential value to him; because that is what I would do for his company. Shaking his hand, I left, putting the ball on top of the other resumes.

Yes, I landed the position. Well aimed creativity and relevant colorfulness set me apart. How can *you* win with an inventive and original sales process? That's a good question to ask, every day!

## Tim G. Carter's Top Money Tip

I wish I could say that every business experience has been profitable, but honestly, I have learned from some unpleasant ones as well.

Many businesses grow themselves out of business. Unfortunately, this is experience talking. I owned a company in the 90s and did exactly that. Because I was under-capitalized to sustain the growth, greedy, acquisitive, mercenary investors stole my company right out from under me.

Still, I learned from this. Incremental growth is sustainable growth. Today, I would rather have slower, steadier growth, than growth not well-planned enough to last. Remember: fires burn out; fields come back. Be a field!

If you achieve rapid growth, that's awesome! Still, take the time to make sure you can sustain it. If you're doing the right things and growth is taking a while, remember, slow grow is not *no grow*. My point? Clarify funding plans and sources before launching expansive, new business goals. Do not assume you will find the money in the middle of your plan. This kind of thinking can kill start-ups and young businesses. Solve the funding first. Yes, it may take a little longer, but even the most amazing vision can turn into a disaster without adequate resources. Plan to win, by winning with your planning.

We must have strong roots to prosper long-term in life and relationships. It is the same in business. Just because others can't see your growth, does not mean you are not growing. Just because you can't point to immediate results, does not mean you are not growing (I am not recommending a lack of initiative). The point is that solid growth usually happens in stages. Some stages are evident to see, and some formative stages are *real*, but not so plain to the eye. Solve your funding issues first. Sizzle! Not Fizzle.

## About Tim G. Carter

Born June 23, 1959, Tim and his wife Dawn have a blended family of six children. He has traveled extensively. Tim is a recorded Quaker Minister, an experienced public speaker, and a sales trainer. His sales success history is life-long and extensive. He is an active outdoorsman, teaches karate, and runs a local business in Thomasville, NC. Tim has sold many millions of dollars through his career. He is currently expanding his public speaking interests.

**Learn more about Tim G. Carter at TimGCarter.com**

# Chapter 2

# ≷Brilliant Tips≶ from Jasmin Christensen

## Jasmin Christensen's Top Mindset Tip

I start each day with a thought as to what I have and where I am. Not the "oh geez" type of thoughts. I truly am grateful for what I have at this very moment and in this place. Yes, I do this mental exercise while brushing my teeth. Next, I go upstairs for coffee. While waiting for the kettle to boil I think of what I want to accomplish for the day. It's a routine that I have found works well for me. Staying in the positive sets the tone for the day.

I think of the negative aspects of any unpleasant chores while I'm in the shower. I know it sounds funny, but as I let the warm water fall over me, I mentally go through the unpleasant chores in my mind. As I'm shampooing my hair, I visualize the negative, unpleasant aspects of those chores. Then I rinse it all away with the shampoo suds. As I finish, I visualize all the positive aspects that will come from completing the unpleasant chores. As I do a final rinse with cold water, it sets the mental positive picture in my mind as surely as the cold water raises goose bumps on my skin. As I'm toweling off, the excitement of the positive builds within me.

What I'm really going for—before I ever set foot in my office—are the positive mental images and feelings that I carry with me throughout the day. No matter what I might be facing, or how unpleasant the chore or task, I always make certain my mindset is positive. Giving in to the negative is guaranteeing failure. A positive mindset will overcome any obstacle, and that's what's needed for a successful business.

## Jasmin Christensen's Top Business Management Tip

Good management is key to the smooth running of any business, big or small. If you're just starting out in business, you can find yourself spending many hours working on multiple small tasks. These may include anything from website maintenance, blog writing, e-mail newsletters, and all of the tasks necessary to keep a small business going. A good friend of mine once told me, "If it's not your genius, it's not your job." What she meant by that was, don't kill yourself with tasks that you aren't good at, when you can outsource.

I know, a small business that is struggling in the beginning may not have lots of funds for hiring. One of my favorite sources for finding wonderfully talented people for very reasonable fees is Fivrr.com. I've personally found web content writers, radio jingle creators, marketing gurus, and website designers. Just be clear about what you want and need.

Another great source of business help is a Virtual Assistant. They can handle lots of things that you might not be a genius at, and they can make your life so much easier. After all, isn't being a good manager all about delegating tasks, so that everything runs much more smoothly? Virtual Assistants, or VA's, can be absolute gems and are worth their weight in gold. A good VA can update your website, write your blogs, publish them for you, update the e-mail newsletters, and put together any number of great projects to help your business stay on top. So, delegate, delegate, delegate!

**Jasmin Christensen's Top Visibility Tip**

Go where the people are! Yes, that means club meetings, high-end coffee shops, and wherever the people are. That can also mean going to large events in your line of business. I like the club meetings, myself. The local *Rotary Club*, *Lion's Club*, and *Kiwanis* are all great organizations, and offer opportunities for you to do a speech or talk on what you have to offer. I don't mean giving a sales pitch to a room of captive people. I mean that you can really educate them about what it is you do, why you are unique, and what you have to offer. I have received several referrals from doing just this sort of thing.

Whenever I go out for errands, or just to get a decent coffee and do some book store perusing, I always have a fresh stock of business cards in my bag. I've gotten clients while waiting to have my tires changed, at the water department counter, and even at my local 24-hour grocery store. Of course, it's amazing what a smile and a pleasant comment can do to break the ice. I always have a tip or two to impart to someone who might be interested. So, don't be afraid to be yourself, make a good first impression, offer a bit of free help if asked, and just enjoy meeting people. Be prepared to meet anyone and everyone. Who knows, you might just get your next referral or speaking gig out of a chance meeting in just about any place. So, get out there and go where the people are.

**Jasmin Christensen's Top Sales Tip**

I'll be perfectly honest, sales has never been a strong suit of mine. So, when I decided to run my own business I had to learn, and fast. This goes back to what a mentor of mine once told me about being willing to invest in self education all the time. If the area of sales was my weak point, then sales was what I was going to learn how to do. I learned something amazing about the sales world, and it had very little to do with the old fashioned, hardcore, pushy sales tactics most people think about. Sales has to do with *love*. Yes, that's right, *love*; love for what you do and the service or product that you offer; and love for the person you are sharing your wonderful gift with. I'm not getting all esoteric on you, by wonderful gift I mean the service or product that you are offering.

Why love? I'll tell you why. If you love what you are doing, then you believe in it, heart and soul. If you believe in what you are offering, then it will show in how you speak and in what you present, and the person you're interacting with can't help but be interested in what has you so enamored. That powerful emotion can't help but become contagious, pushing you to offer better and better services or products, which in turn will gain the attention of more and more people. So, love what you are, what you do, and what you are offering. Plain and simple.

## Jasmin Christensen's Top Money Tip

I heard a very successful entrepreneur say this about money, "Spend less than you earn and save the rest." Now, by ". . . save the rest," he meant that we should invest that money into something that will grow. Most people will agree that investing in your business is always smart, but how many will tell you that investing in yourself *is* investing in your business? That's right, invest in yourself. I don't mean that you should buy a hot new car, or things like that. What I mean is to keep educating yourself and allow that education to help you hone your craft. You are, after all, the biggest and best asset your business has, especially if you are a solopreneur.

For your self-education, attend as many lectures, events, and trainings as you possibly can. At the very least, you should attend one event each quarter, in order to keep yourself at the forefront of your chosen business. Whether it's an onsite event featuring a huge-name presenter or trainer, or an online (virtual) event featuring a speaker few people know, consider getting the training. Many of these training events are priceless and will go far in serving you and your business. So, part of your "savings" should be to invest in yourself, on a regular basis (monthly and quarterly). You will be amazed at how much knowledge you will have gained at the end of the year. Your business will thrive, as you will, with your newly found knowledge and skills. This feeling of self appreciation will transfer over into how you handle your clients. Most people view a business that is "invested in" regularly as something of great value. This helps attract more clients. So, remember, "... Spend less than you earn and save the rest." You and your business are worth the investment, don't you think?

## About Jasmin Christensen

Dr. Jasmin Christensen is the Founder of Healing Connections and Pathways. She began teaching and counseling while on active duty in the USMC. With over 20 years experience, empowerment and healing are the main focus of her work. She has unique experience in trauma related therapy work onsite at disasters (such as 9/11 in NYC). Her ability to help people heal themselves and their lives is her unique niche. Being a Multiple Sclerosis patient herself, she has firsthand experience overcoming almost insurmountable odds daily. Dr. Christensen lectures both nationally and internationally.

## Learn more about Jasmin Christensen at HealingConnectionsAndPathways.com

# Chapter 3

# ≽Brilliant Tips≼ from Rick Cooper

## Rick Cooper's Top Mindset Tip

As an entrepreneur and coach, I have found that many business owners have difficulty staying motivated and on track in building their business. They struggle daily with making progress.

The challenge for many business owners is that they just keep doing the same things and getting the same results. There is a power in consistency. There is also a power in change. My top mindset tip is to set bigger goals in your business.

A goal is a powerful catalyst for change. Your goals will drive your behavior. If there is an area of your business where you are struggling, identify what actions you need to take to create a breakthrough. Then, set a goal that will motivate and inspire you to take those actions.

A few years ago, my business experienced a slowdown. My results decreased and I was enrolling fewer clients. I needed to increase my results. One of the ways to reach more people is by picking up the phone and making calls. I set a goal to make 10 calls a day. That's 50 calls a week. Some people can easily make 40 to 50 calls a day, depending on their workload. 10 was enough for me to make contact, schedule appointments, and begin to create the results I needed.

Is there an area of your business where you are struggling? Think about what worked in the past. Ask others for advice. Set a goal that will help you to get results.

There are certain things you can do that will catapult your business forward. These things are usually out of your comfort zone and require a lot of work to implement. You need to plan, block time, allow time for learning, and seek out supportive mentors to help in accomplishing these goals.

## Rick Cooper's Top Business Management Tip

It takes time and effort to build your business, so be focused and deliberate about what you want to accomplish. How productive are you? Here are some of the activities you can do to market your business online:

- Write blog posts
- Attend online events
- E-mail marketing
- Social media marketing
- Post videos on YouTube
- Publish articles
- Direct mail
- Create a newsletter
- Host a teleseminar or webinar
- Attend trade show events
- Trade show marketing
- Online discussion groups

The question is how many of these activities are you doing and how often are you doing them?

If you want to accomplish more, then you need a way to create more leverage. Leverage is a way to do more with less. For example, you can share an idea with a person one-on-one, and reach that one person with your message. Or, you can record a video and then hundreds or even thousands of people can watch your video. Unfortunately, few business owners actually take the time to record videos.

Leverage your calendar. It's really one of the most underutilized tools. Block time on your calendar for big projects. Block time for planning. And batch tasks.

One of my habits is to plan my day on paper before the day begins. I sit down and write out a plan of action. I write down each of the projects and tasks I need to work on. I also re-write my schedule for the day, blocking time for any special projects I need to devote time to complete.

I use *Google Calendar* to maintain my schedule. I also use a service called *TimeTrade* to book appointments. The benefit is that I can e-mail a link to schedule an appointment with me online. *TimeTrade* looks at my *Google Calendar* and offers time that I am available. Now that's a timesaver!

**Rick Cooper's Top Visibility Tip**

One of the simple online marketing strategies you can implement is to create content. You will position yourself as an expert if you create content and post it online in your area of expertise.

After you post content for a while, you can start seeking out opportunities for publicity. A simple way to create more visibility is through interviews on Internet radio.

What content would you like to create? You can write blog posts and articles. You can record videos. You can also create an information product.

Set up a *Wordpress* blog. Once you have content, there are many ways you can use it. For example, you can share it on social media. I share blog posts on social media including Facebook, Twitter, and LinkedIn. I share my own blog posts, as well as posts from other experts.

Another great technique is to repurpose content. That involves taking content from one form and converting it into another form. For instance, you could take an article you have posted on EzineArticles.com and convert it into a teleseminar script. You might need to expand on the content. You would also want to share more of your personal story at the beginning, and share an offer at the end.

The ultimate way to leverage content is to create an information product you can sell. Not only will it create a new revenue stream, it's a great way to position yourself as an expert and attract clients. This is a larger content project though, and might take three or more months to complete. So, be sure to plan it out and take action each week.

Creating visibility online is easy, but it takes effort and strategy to reach your ideal clients in large numbers. Create and publish content consistently and you will attract clients effortlessly.

## Rick Cooper's Top Sales Tip

Sales is the lifeblood of any business. Earning sales creates ongoing cash flow, so it should be one of your top priorities.

I have studied sales and marketing all of my life. I have read books, listened to audio programs, attended training events, and I have mastered selling skills.

First, remember that selling is more about understanding *people* than it is about understanding your product. You need to be able to connect with people one-on-one or one-to-many to be successful.

My top sales tip is to use sales scripts. Many business owners don't like the idea of using a script because it seems like it is too mechanical. Let me explain why this is such a powerful strategy.

I learned this technique from my mentor Eric Lofholm who learned it from Dr. Donald Moine.

The key idea is to deliver a well prepared, persuasive presentation. Most people wing it. When you wing it, you get wing it results.

In this economy, you have to peak perform. Otherwise, you might as well quit and get a job.

When you script out your presentation, it gives you confidence and the ability to adapt and adjust in the moment when you are meeting with a prospective client.

And don't limit yourself to scripting out your presentation. You can also script responses to common objections or concerns. You see, there is no need to reinvent the wheel. Once you identify a good solution, you can use that solution again in the future.

I have developed multiple sales scripts for my business. It allows me to be prepared during a meeting with a potential client so I can be present with them in the moment rather than in my head.

This could be a million-dollar idea if you implement it.

## Rick Cooper's Top Money Tip

One of the ways to measure success is by how much money you earn and keep. My money tip is a simple one. Don't go into debt and always maintain a cash reserve for your business. For most business owners, the best way to build the business is to bootstrap it. That means start small, earn money, and reinvest it into your business.

Let go of the idea that you need to build your business fast. Unless you are launching a technology company where timing is critical, you will be better off growing slowly and steadily.

It's easy to spend money fast. You need to develop the discipline to spend money wisely in your business.

And don't just spend everything you have. Watch your expenses and build up a cash reserve. How much do you need? It depends on your expenses and your sales cycle. For some $500 to $1,000 may be enough. Others may want to save $5,000 or more.

The purpose of a reserve is to save for a rainy day. And you should have a business reserve and a personal reserve. You don't want to have to raid your business every time you have a past due bill.

Build your business for the long haul. If you are not financially successful in your business, then you might consider straddling. Take a full time job and work your business part time. That would relieve some of the money pressures, and once an entrepreneur, always an entrepreneur. You need to do what you must to take care of your family.

If you currently have debts, consider following a process like the debt snowball to pay off your debts. I learned about this valuable strategy from Financial Expert Dave Ramsey. Make sure you are moving in the right direction.


## About Rick Cooper

Rick Cooper is an online marketing and social media trainer. He works with small business owners who want to generate leads and earn sales online. He specializes in helping entrepreneurs leverage their expertise to attract clients. Rick is founder of *Social Media Outcomes*, based in Sacramento, California, and he is the author of *Seize Your Opportunities, Marketing Magic,* and *Extreme Excellence.* Rick is an international speaker and was featured in *Comstocks Magazine* and interviewed by *The National Networker*.

**Learn more about Rick Cooper at SocialMediaOutcomes.com**

# Chapter 4

## ᶟBrilliant Tipsᶟ from Margo DeGange

### Margo DeGange's Top Mindset Tip

Working in the area of visibility for over 25 years, I'm certain that a good mindset precedes success. It's the energy that triggers positive motion.Without it, business is an uphill climb, into the wind, in the snow, with no shoes, and no hot cocoa!

My top mindset tip is this: *be your own success coach*! I am a big supporter of working with a mentor or coach, or being in a mastermind group with a team of "peer coaches," who spark your creative thinking, help you see golden opportunities, and speak encouragement into your life. It's an empowering gift! Even more empowering though, is having that gift with you at all times, and you do! You can be your own success coach! It involves two important parts: *your walk* and *your talk*!

### *Your Walk:* The Faith-Walk of the Entrepreneur

Did you know that if you're aligned with God (Source), and you have a burning desire for a thing (such as a profitable business, or to do a specific kind of work), then the thing you desire already exists? Yes, it does, because if you're aligned, then that desire was actually put in your heart by God (Source). Even better: if the desire is there, the provision for it is absolutely there, too. Here's how to access it:

1.  Get clear on what you definitively want.

Shut out everything you've falsely told yourself you want, and what others have suggested you might or should want. Life is much too precious and valuable to waste even a fragment of it living a life that's not in line with your own truth or calling. Become acutely aware of *your divine desire*. How? Simply ask yourself, "What do I want?" Listen as the answer comes.

2.   Let go of what's behind.

Ditch the thinking that produced your undesirable results. Open up to something new. Cut the emotional ties to what's not working, and don't go back! Your only option must be something new to get you to your Promised Land (a paradigm shift: a new modality of thinking and believing for new results)!

3.   Take a step, then take the next!

Ask for the first step, then move! It will appear as an opportunity that says, "Take me." Doing so will require you to stretch in some new way, like investing a bit more time, money, energy, or effort than you think you can. You won't experience change and growth if you cling to the comfort of the familiar. Take the step as it appears to you. Stretch into this awesome, new opportunity, then ask for the next step. When it appears, take it. Then ask for another. Each step *will* appear *after* you take the previous step, until you finally realize your goal or desire. *That's* the faith walk of the entrepreneur!

**Your Talk: Speak Encouragement to Yourself**

Your own mouth holds the words of a business coach, a spiritual guru, and a friend! You can speak power to yourself that lifts you out of the muck, and positions you for greatness!

No matter where you are, turn on your power voice! When you're in the shower, sing an uplifting song. In the car, give yourself a motivational speech. When you're waiting for your next client, remind yourself of the value of your skills, products, and services. Speak words of enlightenment and excitement about all that is yours to experience, achieve, and accomplish!

Each day when you awake, speak to yourself with a song, a business principle, a mini-sermon, an *"I've got this,"* and see if it doesn't totally transform the way you live and work.

## Margo DeGange's Top Business Management Tip

If you don't measure it, you can't manage it. My tip here is to *measure everything in your business* to constantly improve. Measure expenses, profits, gross profits, and net profits. Measure gross profit per job or client. Measure which activities get the most and best leads.

Also measure your number of sales per week (month, and year), your number of appointments, how many appointments become sales (closing rate), and your average sale amount.

Measuring allows you to create benchmarks (baselines) over which you can improve. For example, if your measurements reveal your sales are $2000 per week, with a gross profit of 48 percent, you may strategize to make sales of $2500 per week, and a gross profit of 55 percent (gross profit=sales, minus costs associated with sales, excluding regular business expenses).

If measuring and benchmarking seem like big tasks, start small and basic. Begin by setting a few key business goals geared towards making profits (such as your desired yearly sales broken down by week, desired number of appointments and sales, and desired average sale amount). Take the time to measure them on a weekly basis to see how you're doing, and how you can improve to increase profits.

**Margo DeGange's Top Visibility Tip**

Focus and simplify! Create a menu of offerings (products, services, and events). Get a marketing calendar. Put it on your wall. Create four to six marketing campaigns for the year, based on your offerings (the ones on your menu).

Focus all of your marketing time and effort on the current campaign (the sale, promotion, product launch, or event that is coming up on the calendar). Don't even *think* about the next campaign or creating brand new product launches (until the next year). It seems elementary, but few people focus. Instead, they're all over the board selling and marketing without a plan.

For each campaign, choose (in advance) a few marketing activities that have proven most effective for you in the past, and do them with consistency and with a vengeance. Some suggestions might be: social media ads, speaking gigs to make offers, "reach out" phone calls, and direct mail. Use a powerful group of a few, well-focused activities.

**Margo DeGange's Top Sales Tip**

*Focus on the Three Ways to Increase Sales*

The purpose of a business is to make profits. Without them, you've got a hobby. You create profits through sales. Simple!

Many business owners spin their wheels doing all kinds of marketing and management activities, but fail to grow profits by focusing regularly on improving *the only three ways to increase sales*: **appointments**, **closing rate**, and **average sale amount**. You can't increase sales any other way! Focus on improving these, and your profits will fly! Let's look at each:

1.   Appointments

You must get **appointments** to make sales. Based on your financial goals, decide how many appointments you need per month or week. Then, get to work meeting and talking with people to schedule those appointments. To increase your sales and *grow* profits, increase the number of appointments you schedule. Realize though, that there may be a cut-off point where more appointments do not increase sales. Too many appointments can cause your sales conversations to suffer (until you hire and train a sales team).

2. Closing rate (how often you close the sale)

Once you make the appointment to present your products and services to the prospect, you must close the sale. You increase sales and profits by increasing how many prospects you close. What is your closing rate right now? Is it 60 percent, for example (six closes out of ten appointments)? *Know* this number and continuously look for ways to improve it. This may require investing in sales training specific to your industry.

3. Average sale amount

When I owned my Decorating firm, I quickly saw that the easiest way to increase sales was to increase my average ticket. After all, the client (who *chose* to work with me), was right in front of me, ready for additional products to improve their life! So I offered them. Add-on selling became my number one sales tool. I could easily increase almost every job by at least 20 percent without much effort. *Purpose to increase each sale!*

Sales and profits are that simple. Don't complicate it. You don't need a lot of "hoopla" to have good sales. If you're fortunate enough to have a conversation with a prospect, you have the potential to grow your business.

# Margo DeGange's Top Money Tip

## *Value Your Business Currency and Exchange Rate*

Think of your business as a "country," one that people visit for new experiences to enhance their lives. Now, think of your country as having a *currency* and an exchange rate!

Money is something that denotes *value*. It is a type of currency. When you "get" money from a client, you get currency. You also *give* currency in exchange (which is your product or service that improves or enhances the client's life in some way).

If you make the currency you *give* more valuable than what you *get*, you will build a solid business. You'll never have to be concerned that you charge "too much" for your products or services, since your "exchange rate" is always to your client's advantage. In your country, the client always comes out ahead!

## About Margo DeGange

Business and Lifestyle Designer Margo DeGange, M.Ed., is an international best-selling author, sought-after speaker, and the founder of Women of Splendor, the exciting networking and mentoring organization where women collaborate, discover and develop their brilliance, increase their reach and visibility, and bring healing to the world in a BIG and splendid way. Margo is also the founder of Splendor Publishing, where experts become published authors quickly and with ease. Known as *The Visibility Expert*, Margo helps entrepreneurs discover their "Gift of Brilliance" and shine *full throttle*!

**Learn more about Margo DeGange at MargoDeGange.com**

# Chapter 5

# ≥Brilliant Tips≤ from Barbara Drohan Dooley

**Barbara Drohan Dooley's Top Mindset Tip**

Be willing to do something imperfectly for a while. This is what my mentor Lisa Sasevich says. Your best today is good enough. Be willing to accept that while you are learning, what you are creating may not match your dreams.

For most people starting out, there is a performance gap, which feels *terrible*! Truly, it is this feeling that stops many people from moving forward, and ends many dreams. For me, it felt like I was totally off-track, and not capable of achieving my deepest desires. My thought process was that my name is on "this," and I want it to be the *best* of the *best*, and nothing less will do! This caused me to become stagnant, because my experience was not matching my expectations. How can anyone live up to the standard of perfection?

My most important advice; *don't quit*! Close the gap by allowing time for your work to catch up with your dream. "Practice makes perfect" is the old saying, but it does not need to be perfect. With practice and giving it your best, you and your process will certainly get better and better. Perfection can kill the creative process, so be happy with your best today. And, in the process, you learn, grow, and get a greater understanding of not only what you are creating, but of yourself as well. There is incredible richness in the journey.

## Barbara Drohan Dooley's Top Business Management Tip

My top tip here is to measure your progress so things run more smoothly. How many times have you made a decision and the results were not what you expected? After a less than ideal decision, you may even feel further behind than you were before. First, acknowledge your true feelings. Don't ignore them, stuff them, or mask them. Then, see your "mistake" as a necessary step to provide you with the information you need.

If you can change your mindset to see your activity as forward movement, even though it doesn't feel like it, you can use this new information to powerfully move further along on your path, instead of allowing it to stall you. Here are some questions you can ask yourself:

1. "How can I make this work *for* me, even though it's not what I expected?"

2. "What are my options now that I have this new information?"

Stop labeling things as good or bad. Instead of using judgment to knock the legs out from under you, decide what to do next from a positive perspective and consider asking, "What can I do differently here that would get me to my desired results?" Use your frustration and possible disappointment as an opportunity to move forward to new, more desirable results.

## Barbara Drohan Dooley's Top Visibility Tip

What really works for me in the realm of visibility in marketing is to go to functions, classes, and activities that I really enjoy, and let the conversation flow naturally. Many of my clients have similar interests to mine, and when the conversation flows from the heart in a casual, relaxed setting, people can see the real value offered.

A slight spin on this idea is to find out where your ideal client hangs out, and look for opportunities and ways to connect. It doesn't always have to be at a networking event or a formal function. I do *not* have sales conversations at any event, but I do take their card and contact them in the next day or so to have a full conversation about what their needs are, and if they match up with what I have to offer. This eases any discomfort with marketing because I am relaxed and having fun!

I was recently at a concert in a beautiful outdoor setting, and I started chatting with a gal who I didn't know, and she asked me what I do for a living. In the end, she took my card and we really connected. See opportunities everywhere you go, and connect with others from the heart.

## Barbara Drohan Dooley's Top Sales Tip

Always be thinking about "what is in it for them" and approach the sales conversation with an attitude of fun and light-heartedness. Ask quality, insightful questions and listen deeply to uncover if they are an ideal client for you, and if you can serve them fully. This approach eliminates pursuit and desperation, making hardcore sales a thing of the past. Relax into the process and share from your heart, authentically, by telling them that you have been where they are now, and that you have an answer for them (and only if that is the truth, of course, otherwise refer them to someone you know can help). Coming from the mindset of "Let's explore this together" versus "What can I get" develops an authentic connection where a person can see that you are real and they can trust you. From this platform, they feel safe and can make a decision from their heart, and from the power that exists in the moment between both of you. The mind conjures up too many excuses and ways to look for an out, especially if this is a growth opportunity that might frighten them. Be authentic and make a heart connection and your work with them will be just what you dreamed it to be.

## Barbara Drohan Dooley's Top Money Tip

Be grateful for what you already have. When you come from this place, your heart is more open to receive. Set your intention every day to notice and appreciate five things that you are grateful for. It is thinking about what you *do* have versus what you don't have that will begin to open the door for a powerful shift in perspective. There is a part of our brain called the *Reticular Activating System*. Its job is to bring to you more of what you are already focused on. So, what are you focused on? Do you want what you already have? Do you need to shift your focus? What do you really want? Focus on that, and things will start to change for you. Along the way, your old patterns and beliefs will come into your awareness, which brings you to a powerful choice point. What do you *really* want? Do you want to repeat the patterns of the past or do you want to live from the power of the present and create something new? Be grateful for how the past has brought you to where you are today, look at your fears, and appreciate them for what they have taught you, and choose differently.

## About Barbara Drohan Dooley

Barbara Drohan Dooley is a Clarity Consultant, speaker and teacher, who works with people who feel they are settling for less than they deserve in life, helping them to move into a rich and fulfilling life experience.

Barbara is a certified Consulting Hypnotist and teacher of self hypnosis, with training in Emotional Freedom Technique, Neuro-linguistic Programming, and many other energy modalities. Barbara works with people world wide to bring them home to themselves.

## Learn more about Barbara Drohan Dooley at SoulRemembrance.com

# Chapter 6

# ≷Brilliant Tips≶ from Patty Farmer

**Patty Farmer's Top Mindset Tip**

I believe that mindset accounts for 80 percent of our business success, and our skill-set accounts for 20 percent. As solo-entrepreneurs, we too often get in our own way when we have self-sabotaging conversations with ourselves. Some of these self-sabotaging thoughts may include:

- ≷ I can't afford it
- ≷ I don't have the time
- ≷ I'm not smart enough
- ≷ I don't know enough
- ≷ I don't know how to create products
- ≷ I'm uncomfortable with what to charge for my products and services

Any one of these self-sabotaging mindsets can prevent you from achieving your business goals. Changing your mindset is critical for success, and some changes can happen sooner than others!

How do you change a mindset that is sabotaging you? The first step is to write down what you know is causing you issues, and then take a look at *why* you tend to think that way. Think of some possible ways to change your negative thinking habit. Try out different solutions and different ways of thinking about your obstacles and about your business. When one doesn't work, try another.

If you have multiple mindset shifts you wish to make, focus on only one each month, and put all of your effort into making that one change. Create a new habit.

Sometimes, it is wise to invest in yourself. Resources such as a life or business coach, books (check out how cognitive therapy techniques can be used at home/work to change your self-talk and mindset), and other resources can help you create change, and often much more speedily than without them.

Creating a positive mindset in your personal and business life will increase the quality of your life and around!

## Patty Farmer's Top Business Management Tip

As individuals, we all have gifts or brilliance in certain areas. When we are allowed to focus on these, our businesses can do amazing things. Unfortunately, the details of running a business can get in the way.

Your business will excel if the systems and infrastructure are there to support both it and you. Having a team that creates and supports a good foundation—so that you can focus on your brilliance—is what will take your business to the next level.

Creating a support team starts small and grows, but you *do* have to find the time and money to create your team (even when you just don't think you can). Your goal should be to free up your time from the details of running your business, so you can focus on growing your business instead. Start by clearly identifying the services that you need. Then, set out to find the "right" people for the job. Also, realize that free, cheap, or bartering aren't always the best avenues to pursue.

Eventually, invest in a business manager who will be your pivot (the one-touch person you deal with) who will manage all the sources needed to get your projects done. Dealing with only one point person makes life much easier. You don't have to hire people full-time. Have multi-talented people available, and always have an operational manual that is up-to-date. In addition, utilizing a project management system is a very wise investment.

To create a successful business, you cannot be the only person working on it. Unfortunately, too many entrepreneurs do just that. It takes a team of people with different skills to build your business; this also allows you to focus your time on the tasks only you can do.

## Patty Farmer's Top Visibility Tip

I invite you to reconsider how you think about podcasting! Having your own podcast show increases your visibility not only through listeners, but through the various guests you showcase.

When you attend networking functions, conferences, or events, you have a great opportunity to meet people and invite them to be on your podcast show.

You can also have them write a guest blog for you, and you can further expand your visibility by having a custom tab on your Facebook business page to drive traffic to your website. On your website, you can feature a page about your podcast.

You can promote your podcast and guests through social media platforms as well as through their guest blog, which will give you visibility through their network, through social sharing, and through your blog.

Next, you can add your podcasts to *iTunes*, which is a key clearinghouse for podcasts, and is where hundreds of thousands of people go to access podcasts of interest to them.

A big benefit too, is that through meeting and networking with your podcast show guests, you create a list of people to pull from when you put on your own event, and need speakers and promotional partners.

## Patty Farmer's Top Sales Tip

### *Serve Not Sell!*

After a closing question is asked, the first person who talks loses! What this means is that once you make your sales presentation, wait until the customer speaks. Why? Because if you speak, you are likely to leave the door open for the customer to make excuses and demands.

When you go to a store to buy something, you see their prices and you have to decide to pay those prices or not. Your business services and products have worth, and you've priced them accordingly. The customer has to decide whether or not to buy your product or service for what they are priced.

If you start negotiating because a customer wants a lower price, and if you give in to that kind of pressure, you are disrespecting yourself and your business.

The most important thing to do is to change your mindset from selling to serving. If you have created a relationship with a potential customer based on integrity; if you have listened intently; if you asked the "right" questions; if you came up with good, strategic solutions to meet your customer's needs, then the sale will naturally occur.

Remember—Serve Not Sell!

## Patty Farmer's Top Money Tip

Many business owners find pricing their services and products difficult. It starts with creating value. Through research of similar services and products, finding an initial pain-point for your audience can be accomplished. Knowing your target market's concerns, desires, and preferences, you can create quality products and services that meet and exceed their needs and expectations.

Belief in the value of what you have created will allow you to set prices you feel comfortable with, and will ensure that confidence in your pricing comes across when you are speaking to potential customers. One of my favorite quotes is, *"The only function price serves is to set the expectation of value"* -Alicia Arenas.

### *Invest in Yourself*

Your number one client is yourself! Taking care of you is crucial if your business is going to flourish. This involves learning the right strategies and techniques that will help you to manage your time, reduce stress, prevent burnout, create balance in your life, and invest in yourself.

Investing in yourself is not just about getting sub-contractors to help you grow your business. It also means investing resources to attend events where you can learn and network, as well as investing in books, audios, and other products for business and personal growth. Investing in coaching for yourself and for your business can create dramatic change in your business too.

As entrepreneurs, we are usually busy trying to meet the needs of others, and putting out fires as our first priorities. In reality, our first priority is to take care of our number one client—ourselves! The key is to work on increasing your business and income, without getting trapped in doing what others want you to do.

## About Patty Farmer

Patty Farmer, The Networking CEO™, is a multi-award winning and highly sought after Marketing and Business Growth Strategist, International Speaker, Trainer, Radio Show Host, and Bestselling Author.

Patty has created a network of 100,000 + connections while teaching thousands of business owners how to effectively network, build their list, fill their marketing funnel, and create key positioning techniques to grow their businesses using a non-competitive and dynamic collaboration strategy.

**Learn more about Patty Farmer at PattyFarmer.com**

# Chapter 7

# ⸗Brilliant Tips⸗ from Carla Ferrer

## Carla Ferrer's Top Mindset Tip

Often, we mistakenly attribute business success to the innate abilities of those who achieve it. We assume that the skills of a Henry Ford, a Steve Jobs, or a Jeff Bezos are somehow hardwired into their DNA. I believe that the real secret of success resides in people's mindset, in that a "fixed" mindset that ascribes success to innate qualities, is less resilient and adaptable than a "growth" mindset that connects achievement to continuous learning and persistence.

Thus, the simple distinction between labeling oneself as successful or unsuccessful and labeling our performance as successful or unsuccessful can make all the difference as you strive to meet tomorrow's challenges.

In as much, your attitude rubs off on your existing and potential customers, your staff, your suppliers, your investors and all those that you come into contact with.

If you maintain a positive attitude, this will be infectious, and those around you will pick up on your positive energy. Everyone in your company will feel positive and customers will want to do business with you. This in turn will lead to you maximizing the performance of your business.

If you maintain a negative attitude, the opposite is likely to happen. People will not want to be around you, your staff will feel unmotivated, and customers will not want to buy from you.

The result will be that the performance of your business will deteriorate.

With a positive approach you will feel in control and confident, and you will perform at your best, whereas a negative approach will damage confidence, harm performance, paralyze your mental skills, and may also impact your health.

Simply stated, attitude is key; and truly embracing and/or implementing practices that help you maintain a cool and calm demeanor as you go about your day, will result quite favorably for you in a multitude of ways over time.

## Carla Ferrer's Top Business Management Tip

### *Leadership*

You cannot expect your team to be innovative if they do not know the direction in which they are headed. Innovation has to have a purpose. It is up to the leader to set the course and give a bearing for the future. You need one overarching statement which defines the direction for the business and which people will readily understand and remember. Great leaders spend time illustrating the vision, the goals, and the challenges. They explain to people how their role is crucial in fulfilling the vision and meeting the challenges. They inspire men and women to become passionate entrepreneurs finding innovative routes to success.

Great suggestion schemes are focused, easy to use, well-resourced, responsive, and open to all. They do not need to offer huge rewards. Recognition and response are generally more important. Above all, they have to have the whole-hearted commitment of the senior team to keep them fresh, properly managed and successful.

## Carla Ferrer's Top Visibility Tip

### *Utilizing and Maximizing Social Media*

If you're looking for a new way to attract quality leads using social media, try *Facebook Offers*.

*Facebook Offers* are a type of Facebook ad, but they work a bit differently than a traditional Facebook ad. You can set them up directly from your Facebook page (no need to go into the Ads dashboard) and they can be created for offline and online businesses.

Although you can use them for many different promotions, I've seen the highest conversion rates when marketers use *Facebook Offers* to attract quality leads.

My biggest tip is strategic: combine all the best of digital marketing by maximizing social media.

If you use SEO, organic social media, search advertising, social advertising, and Google remarketing ads, then you're doing the best of everything.

You're raising awareness for new business via Facebook, you're getting the low-hanging fruit of buying-intent keywords via Google, and you're making sure that people who've been to your site keep seeing you via Google remarketing and your Facebook fan base.

## Carla Ferrer's Top Sales Tip

### *Sales Funnels and Successful Closes*

Qualification is the most critical and demanding stage of the sales funnel. In the qualification process, you verify that the prospect has a need for your product, that the prospect sees value in your offering, that there is sufficient budget for a deal, that you have access to the decision-maker, and that there is an agreed-upon timeline for the sales process. The qualification process can be complex and lengthy, and can be managed with a good sales call tracking system; for there's no doubt about it, fortune lays in the follow-up!

Ideally, you want to close the deal when all red flags have been dealt with. In reality, most deals close while critical red flags still exist. At this point, you have provided the customer with a proposal that outlines key contractual terms. When a customer has agreed to move forward with a deal, they are "committed" (also known as "verbal commitment" or "verbal"). What remains is to work out the details of the contract, delivery, and payment, all of which have the potential to "undo" the commitment. The commitment may be offered contingent upon certain terms being met.

## Carla Ferrer's Top Money Tip

### *Prosperity Comes by Way of Planning, Preparing and Patience*

In business, there are no guarantees. There is simply no way to eliminate all the risks associated with starting a small business, but you can improve your chances of success with good planning, preparation, and insight. Start by evaluating your strengths and weaknesses as a potential owner and manager of a small business. Carefully consider each of the questions below:

1. Are you a self-starter?

It will be entirely up to you to develop projects, organize your time, and follow through on details.

2. How well do you get along with different personalities?

Business owners need to develop working relationships with a variety of people including customers, vendors, staff, bankers, and professionals such as lawyers, accountants, or consultants.

3. Can you deal with a demanding client, an unreliable vendor, or a cranky receptionist if your business interests demand it?

4. How good are you at making decisions? Small business owners are required to make decisions constantly, and often quickly, independently, and under pressure.

5. Do you have the physical and emotional stamina to run a business?

Business ownership can be exciting, but it's also a lot of work. Can you face six or seven twelve-hour workdays every week?

6. How well do you plan and organize?

Research indicates that poor planning is responsible for most business failures. Good organization—of financials, inventory, schedules, and production—can help you avoid many pitfalls.

7. Is your drive strong enough?

Running a business can wear you down emotionally. Some business owners burn out quickly from having to carry all the responsibility for the success of their business on their own shoulders. Strong motivation will help you survive slowdowns and periods of burnout.

8.   How will the business affect your family?

The first few years of business start-up can be hard on family life. It's important for family members to know what to expect and for you to be able to trust that they will support you during this time. There also may be financial difficulties until the business becomes profitable, which could take months or years. You may have to adjust to a lower standard of living or put family assets at risk in the short term.

In closing, let me be very clear, I firmly believe and know that it's possible that you can genuinely help others, prosper financially, and experience real freedom in your life when you follow your gut, listen to your heart, and cast your fears aside to pursue a business that is true to your passion, and wherein you are sincerely seeking to be of service to others. In doing so, rest assured and know that your just rewards will undoubtedly come over time.

**About Carla Ferrer**

Carla Ferrer is an Author, Entrepreneur, Keynote Speaker, and Nerium International Brand Partner.

As a seasoned Life Coach and Entrepreneur in the field of transformation and consciousness for healthy and affluent lifestyle living, Carla has over 20 yrs of experience empowering profound personal and professional breakthroughs for individuals throughout the United States & United Kingdom.

Carla marries her depth of wisdom and insight, with passion, humor and sensitivity to empower individuals in living a life by design that is rich and strong in every way.

**Learn more about Carla Ferrer at CarlaFerrer.com**

# Chapter 8

# ≥Brilliant Tips≤ from Steve Gutzler

Having the privilege of working and coaching with leading entrepreneurs, fortune 500 companies, CEOs and presidents, along with professional athletes, I feel the tips I am able to offer are not just my own collection, but include those I have gathered from observing world class entrepreneurs and personal leaders.

## Steve Gutzler's Top Mindset Tip

Without a doubt the number one tip I offer is the right mindset . . . a growth mindset.

Everything rises or falls upon our thoughts. I fight daily for a growth mindset. People with a growth mindset don't just seek challenge, they thrive on it. The bigger the challenge, the more they stretch.

A fixed mindset drifts toward being a victim. Every day I get up, I refuse to fall prey to being a victim. I learned a valuable lesson going on a kayaking trip with 32 burn victims two summers ago. I was to provide the inspirational talks to these amazing people. They had burns over 30-95 percent of their bodies. Horrible scarring. On the first evening, as I mentioned how inspired I was by their lives . . . being burn victims, a young man raised his hand and said, "Steve, we never refer to ourselves as victims. We are survivors."

*Yes*, survivors, even *thrivers!* Every day I get up I say, "Steve, today you will survive and thrive in business. Let's go!" Have a growth mindset—play up and always play at your best!

## Steve Gutzler's Top Business Management Tip

Team-up! Resist the temptation of isolation and flying solo. Ideas and production multiply the moment you team-up with others. Just minutes ago I was meeting with an amazing friend who launched a marketing firm. Our lunch was a simple "reach out" by me to hear what he does. Within minutes of our conversation, we were story-boarding ideas for my leadership company. You could feel the mutual energy and quickening pulses as we brainstormed ideas.

One phrase I always try to frame up my conversations around is . . . "It's possible!" Too many entrepreneurs and business owners cancel possibilities by focusing on what is impossible . . . cost, resources, lack of marketing, or dollars. Focus instead on what is possible. Team up with idea people, innovators in the industry, doers, goal setters, and goal getters.

One of my favorite stories in the Bible is the one about the little boy who brought five loaves of bread and two fish to Christ. Talk about teaming up! As they started to pass out the loaves and fish to the multitudes of people, they multiplied and fed over 5000. I'm convinced as we team up, remarkable multiplication occurs.

Your best ideas are yet to be discovered as you begin to build an unstoppable dream team. Make a point of reaching out to someone today! Don't wait—success will come your way!

## Steve Gutzler's Top Visibility Tip

Social media! Think how our world has changed . . . *your* world, with the explosion of social media! Now we have Facebook, Twitter, YouTube, LinkedIn, and other revolutionary platforms. As you know, most are free, but here's the catch . . . you'll either use social media in a smart way, or not!

Think of your business going from local, to global. You have a personal brand which can be visibly displayed on the platforms of social media. I would suggest you play in one or two social media platforms strongly. If its Twitter or Facebook, engage and have content to share that meets a need, want, or desire. In regards to social media, practice the 80/20 rule. 80 percent of your interaction should be engagement and social sharing, and 20 percent can be offers for your services or products.

With everything visible you put out, do your best to represent your brand integrity. I'd rather do less with credible quality, than with visibility that weakens my message.

I meet twice a month with a couple of Internet/social media experts who help me stay current and pressing on the edge of growth.

On a final note around social media, take some time to think through your purpose and a thoughtful strategy. It will serve you in the long run to create purposeful visibility.

## Steve Gutzler's Top Sales Tip

*Trifecta*: a powerful combo of three sales strategies that work in harmony creating an upward spiral of sales.

First is a content based e-news or e-blast, displayed and captured on one page via your computer screen or mobile device. A small box with a link on the bottom or side takes them to your product or service. It could be a separate flyer or page to your side which outlines your program.

Second is a social media post via Facebook, Twitter, LinkedIn, and other social media platforms that comes out within 24-98 hours of your e-news.

Third involves personal calls, texts, and e-mails to potential clients and customers. There is a good chance you caught their eyeballs and have already set the stage for a conversation regarding your business meeting their needs, wants, and desires. Usually over 60 percent of potential clients I contact say, "Hey, I just saw that on Facebook and I received your e-news . . . good stuff!"

I much prefer my trifecta strategy over cold-calls or reaching out to someone without my content-based materials to gain trust and respect. I try to do one quality trifecta every 45 to 60 days!

In addition to the trifecta, here's a little *bonus tip* that I do weekly and that you too, could also easily do. When I look at my schedule for the week, I select one day to contact past clients. It may be a different day each week, depending on my schedule. On that day, I set aside one hour—from 10am to 11am—and I make calls to my past clients to stay well connected. If they are not available by phone, I send them a quick e-mail. This helps keep the relationship strong and keeps the door open for future sales.

## Steve Gutzler's Top Money Tip

Accomplishments! A few years ago in the middle of the "great recession," I slowly slid into a bad habit. Having experience more than my fair share of "No" or "Thanks Steve, not right now," I got a bad case of sales reluctance. My once confident self became gun-shy. Here's the bad habit: I got busy.

Not around accomplishments, but around activities. I started filling my days and calendar with busy work so I would not hear "No."

Finally, I woke up. I now have a daily mantra on my desk. It reads, "M.V.P." which represents my most valuable and profitable use of time. Every day, I try to do at least one thing toward an accomplishment that equals making money.

The way I got over sales reluctance? I got mad! I got good—dare I say great—at new presentations and new marketing that put a little swagger back in my game. Let's face it. Confidence *is* the game. If I feel iconic, kind of like a movie star, well look out, success is coming my way!

. . . and accomplishments? High-value work is the game-changer for me. Money is up and activities are down.

**About Steve Gutzler**

Steve Gutzler is one of the nation's premier thought leaders on leadership, emotional intelligence, and personal transformation. As President of Leadership Quest, a coaching services firm that helps organization grow leaders at every level, he's worked with many Fortune 500 firms including Microsoft, Boeing, and Starbucks. He also works individually with CEOs, business executives, and leading entrepreneurs. Steve has developed effective presentations on team-building, customer service, and emotional intelligence for today's leaders.

**Learn more about Steve Gutzler at SteveGutzler.com**

# Chapter 9

## ⸗Brilliant Tips⸗ from Leslie Hassler

**Leslie Hassler's Top Mindset Tip**

*Take Out the Mind Trash!*

Whether or not you enjoy the success of building your business will be determined by one thing, your mindset. It determines whether you rejoice in the glory of success or languish in the fires of survivorship. My tip is to not treat "mindset" as a to-do item that you have to cross off. Instead, think of it as a recurring tip or cleaning.

To put it simply, if you are an adult venturing into business, you are going to need to do some house cleaning and take out your mind trash in order to be successful. Over the course of your life, your mind has been depositing trash in your possibility room. Sometimes it's just a used napkin, sometimes it's a whole party worth of trash. Your mind makes a trash deposit consciously and unconsciously. It could be from comparison, from judgment, or just general doubt, but every negative conversation dumps more and more trash into your possibility room. Pretty soon, you can't see any more possibilities, you feel defeated, deflated, and lost.

The solution—take out the mind trash! Clean out your possibility room, just as you have to clean your office and your home on a daily and weekly basis. Realize that you have to do the same cleaning with your mindset. The first time is always a killer. Some days it's one bag of "mind trash," and other days there are more. Be consistent. As soon as you see the mind trash in your possibility room, take it to the curb!

## Leslie Hassler's Top Business Management Tip

Multi-tasking is a *myth*! The greatest lie to our society is the concept of multi-tasking. As an entrepreneur, multi-tasking will work for a while, but only until you get busy. What you will find then is that mistakes start to happen, clients get upset, and your brain becomes "fried." Your once productive day becomes a day of putting out fires. The transformation from chaos to control happens by adding a layer of structure to your day.

Start by reducing your interruptions and block your time. Silence the phone, turn off e-mail notifications—be present with the task at hand. Block your day so that it works for your business. If you need open office time—schedule it and let everyone know what time they can see you. Then, work your time blocks. First, do all of your two-minute tasks. Then move on to delegation tasks—information or next steps that require another person to move forward. I like getting this done early in the morning, because I can follow up on them in the afternoon. Then move into project work—time when you have disciplined yourself to work on your business, a client project, or revenue generating work. Whatever the project is, it needs a block of time. It takes an hour just to get into the flow. I like to set aside two hours or more to work on a single project. I then take lunch, and repeat in the afternoon.

At the end of the day, write down your top three things that you need to do tomorrow and any other project related notes. The key is to get it out of your head and onto paper. Your day will be more productive and your mind will be free for the evening.

## Leslie Hassler's Top Visibility Tip

My best marketing visibility tip is to only be visible where testing and measuring makes sense to be visible. Determining where to put your marketing efforts involves a bit of knowing where your clients are, but it has more to do with figuring out what you do well, what's the best use of your time, and which activities have the best return. Every marketing technique has a place and a person that it works for—you need to figure out what your technique is for your business. Every person will tell you that the secret is networking, or referrals, or direct mail. The true key is to find out which marketing method works best for *you*, and then be consistent, and give the marketing a chance to work.

Finding out what works best for you is only done by testing and measuring—tracking the details, how many leads, how many sales, how much in sales. Don't just guess which marketing message is going to work. Take the time to test messages/methods and find out how people respond.

Why is consistency important? Too often, people try a marketing technique once, and when it doesn't work, the proclamation is that the technique doesn't work. Be a mad scientist, experiment on a small scale and find out what works. The knowledge you gain will be your own golden nugget. No one says it will be easy, but imagine figuring out the key messages that your clients will respond to over and over—that's the true secret to marketing. That's the way to catapult your marketing efforts.

## Leslie Hassler's Top Sales Tip

One of the best sales tips I can give you, is to train yourself to identify different personality types within a few minutes of meeting someone new. There are many options, but one of the best is the DISC profile. By learning the four types of personalities, you will be able to identify a personality type by asking a few questions, or by picking up on the words used by your prospect.

When you identify your prospect's personality type, you will understand how your prospect needs to hear information and what information is important to them. It is really a communication strategy. If you have a sales script that only highlights how quickly your product can be delivered (a D concept when using DISC profiles) to a persona that is more concerned with guarantees and safety (a C concept), you are going to have a hard time with your sales conversation. You might as well try selling ice to Eskimos.

If instead, you could anticipate what that C persona really needs to hear is, "You know—there's no pressure here—we believe in our product so much that we guarantee you will be satisfied, or we will refund you 100 percent, " you would experience the impact that would have on your sales.

The best way to communicate is to meet your prospects where they are. The best way to sell is to speak their language. The best way to make the sale is to tell them how your product addresses their concerns. The benefit to you is a high conversion of sales, feeling good while you are selling, and having happy clients who feel you met their needs.

## Leslie Hassler's Top Money Tip

My number one money tip is to know your numbers. Let me be honest, I hate accounting, financial reporting, spreadsheets, and the like. The best way to have control of your money and to grow your money is to *know* your money. My number one tool is a cash flow report. I do mine in Excel—it forces me to really look at the numbers and add them all up. I set up my cash flow report to tell me two things:

1.  Actuals. This lets us look at business committed, money in, and money out. Everything is there: supplies, COGS, and sales tax. I can input in my checking account balance for the week, and it will show me what my cash flow looks like this week, this month, and in three months. I can foresee any shortfalls, decide to get more sales, delay a purchase, etc.

2.  Forecast. The pie-in-the-sky! This is the budget, that is, my goals. Again, everything is here. I can see my sales goals for any period of time. If I want to do a capital expenditure, or plan for a vacation, or hire a new employee, this is the document that tells me what I need my sales to be in order to say "yes."

It is important to review and update your cash flow on a weekly basis. This will eventually become a 30 minute task, but it might take you an hour initially. Getting to know your numbers will give you power to make decisions on sales to close, marketing dollars to spend, and employees to hire. Start off with a 90-day cash flow, and as you get to know your business, you may want to have one that is six months, and ideally, one year out.

## About Leslie Hassler

The CEO- Mindset™ system helps business owners and entrepreneurs, like you, regain the joy in your life and business by finding direction in your child-like dreams, gain confidence and traction through seizing the day and catapulting yourself from the "fires of surviving" in business into the "glories of success".

Leslie Hassler is a speaker, award-winning entrepreneur and founder of the CEO-Mindset™ system.

**Learn more about Leslie Hassler at CEO-Mindset.com**

# Chapter 10

# ≥Brilliant Tips≤ from Julie M. Holloway

## Julie M. Holloway's Top Mindset Tip

Trust your *vision*. At times it may not seem that you are still headed in the right direction, or that everything that "should be" is on track. That's ok. Your vision is so grand, sometimes you just need to step back and trust in it.

Stop and look at your vision from a far, take a look at the entire landscape and meditate in it. Have faith in it, and believe that the end result is achievable.

Running a business is a monstrous responsibility. The key to having and living the right mindset is constantly looking in the mirror and telling yourself that you can do it. Tell yourself you have been called to do this. Tell yourself you have everything you need, and that you will do nothing other than win.

A mentor of mine recently told me to stand in the mirror and give myself a pep talk before a large speaking engagement. The words I spoke unto myself truly gave me the confidence and vision needed to carry my thoughts that day. Although you will have strong supporters in your corner and in your business, you must be the strongest one of all. Be your biggest fan and wake up each morning reiterating to yourself that you are placed here to conquer everything you set out to do.

Just remember that mindset and taking action, are two of the biggest choices you have each morning. Wake up and set your mind right for the day!

## Julie M. Holloway's Top Business Management Tip

In the sea of business management tips that are floating around, the biggest and best in my book is *collaboration*. Your business cannot run for too long with just one person. You are a specialist in a specific area, one where your skills shine. Don't let growth kill you!

Most people are not experts in every single skill (ranging from management, administration, finance, and operations, to customer service, marketing, sales, and accounting), so why try to do it all? In business, collaboration creates better results, it saves time, eliminates waste, and most of all, it increases productivity if done with excellence and the right team.

Start with baby steps and begin to build a team around the brand that you have created. Employ, inspire, and allow others to help you carry the vision and mission of your company to its greatest heights. Some of the most successful entrepreneurs—even those who started as a one man show—have achieved greatness by learning to lead a world-class team.

One of the key ingredients in being a great entrepreneur is sharpening your leadership and management skills so that you can grow your organization. Lead by example, lead with courage, and lead with the desire to help your team achieve their desired goals and dreams. Together you will go far, if you learn to let go and grow!

## Julie M. Holloway's Top Visibility Tip

If you *stop* marketing, they *stop* watching. Always wear your marketing hat, even when you are busy building other aspects of your business. Yes, we know you are busy, however it is vital to keep your businesses heartbeat pumping with brilliant and creative marketing campaigns. Ensure that you are being a "social entrepreneur" by getting out to events, marketing via an e-mail marketing tool such as Constant Contact, and marketing daily via social media platforms such as Facebook, Twitter, and LinkedIn. Social media allows your business network to grow and expand, while networking in person allows you hundreds of opportunities to share what your business does, what your vision is for growth, and what your strategy is to secure clientele. No matter how busy you get, how crazy life may seem, it is vital to market your business every day. Some say it's important to talk about your business at least three times per day to keep a solid pipeline. Whether you are a solopreneur or a business owner with a team, ensure that someone is keeping up with the marketing end of things. It's vital for the voice of your brand to remain active in the marketplace so that you are constantly conversing with current and future clientele.

## Julie M. Holloway's Top Sales Tip

In sales, my motto is *follow up, follow through and follow your heart*. Sales are what keep you in business. It is critical to follow up with potential clients. Invest in a tool or use the simple but effective Google Calendar to trigger follow-up notes and calls. If you don't follow up, why should the client?

Follow up immediately after meeting someone. Don't wait a week; it may be too late! Follow-through is critical in business. There have been occasions when I did not follow through appropriately with a project or a sales lead, and it likely led to lost revenue.

Following your heart is critical. As they say, not all money is good money. Not all clients are good for you. If something in your heart tells you that a client or opportunity is not good for you and your business, do not feel obligated to take it. Many times folks are driven by dollar signs, and choose to ignore what is in their heart. On the occasions I have done this, I have regretted it later because it resulted in a crazy or out of control client. Listen to your heart when making those sales!

## Julie M. Holloway's Top Money Tip

I recently read a book called *Running Lean,* and it sparked some great thoughts and plans for my own business. One of the critical elements of running your business is deciding whether you will be bootstrapping it or seeking outside funding.

Bootstrapping is when you run your business without capital or funding from other sources. You are basically putting everything you have into it, and while you make money, the same money is also going back into the various areas of the business that require an investment.

The other option of course is to seek capital, raise funding, and accept investments from outside parties. I do see the value of both of these methods, however be sure to do your homework. Raising capital from outside sources can be a very lengthy process that takes a lot of time. You may not see eye to eye with the investors, and sometimes it can leave your business with too much money. Of course, one could ask how you could have too much money. Well, if you receive a very large amount in investments, and are unable to fiscally pay back what you owe (through the revenues you are bringing in), you could find yourself in a tight spot with your investors. My advice in this area is to really evaluate the options that you are seeking for your business, and discuss them with a close confidante or business partner. Don't make a huge money decision on a whim; evaluate first.

## About Julie M. Holloway

Julie M. Holloway is a multi-passion creative author, graphic designer, and artist based in Chicago. In 2011, she opened JMH Cre8ive Solutions, and published a book titled *The Entrepreneur Within You*, an inspiring business anthology. With an enormous heart and hunger for collaborating and assisting entrepreneurs to carry through their creative vision, the business continues to flourish. Julie loves spending family time with her husband Darnell and children, Jasmine and DJ.

**Learn more about Julie M. Holloway at JMHCre8ive.com**

# Chapter 11

## ≳Brilliant Tips≲ from Marybeth Hrim

**Marybeth Hrim's Top Mindset Tip**

In all my years of business, looking back I sure wish I would have had a book on this very subject. How many times in business and in life have you failed?

Has your failure created feelings of dread, or has your failure been a piece of opportunity?

A healthy mindset is the most crucial area in business. A great friend once told me that awareness is 50 percent of solving any problem. Awareness is the key that unlocks who you are, what you think, and how you behave.

What is the belief you have about you? What you tell yourself on a daily basis can make or break your confidence. In order to have a healthy bit of confidence, you must be aware of the thoughts that zigzag through your mind. If you tell yourself you don't fit the image of something, then you won't. If you say to yourself, "I am worthy to do this type of work," then you will be. What we say to ourselves has a big impact on what others say. You talk to *yourself* more times in a day than does anyone else you come in contact with. What you tell yourself will be projected onto others. Be aware of what goes on in your head. Mindset is like food. What you feed yourself in thoughts, and how you nourish yourself in thoughts, can help you toward growth and success. What you tell yourself will bring either peace or disarray in your life and business. It all begins with an awareness of how you talk to yourself.

So again, *what* are you telling yourself on a daily basis? Unfortunately, we often talk very negatively to ourselves. We average over 50,000 thoughts per day. How many of those are positive? Imagine if most of those 50,000 thoughts were affirming thoughts? We would be confident, happy, and full of joy.

The first step to healthy thinking is recognizing what kind of an environment you are in. I had a client who began her day with daily affirmations. This would put her in a positive frame of mind, but her environment at work and at home were very negative. Everyone talked about one another behind their backs. The atmosphere was uneasy and chaotic, making it uncomfortable for everyone. She soon realized this was not the place for her, and she had to make a tough choice to leave.

What is your environment like? You must take inventory of that and take care of yourself. If you don't take care and nurture you, no one will. Be kind to you, and if the environment is toxic, make the decision to move on and move forward. You will receive much more respect by moving forward than you will by staying and hoping it will get better. You will feel much better about you and the situation.

Consider keeping a journal of thoughts to help you change negative thoughts into positive ones. This will not only increase your confidence in business, but will help you become a very joyful person! Change your mindset through awareness, and you and your business will be healthier for it.

## Marybeth Hrim's Top Business Management Tip

Whether you're just starting your business or have been in business for some time, it is vitally important that your business has systems. Systems are foundational.

You must be clear on how your product or service will be delivered. This should be well thought out so you are able to deliver in the event of an overabundance of unexpected clients. Always expect the unexpected, and create a solid foundation from which to serve.

A colleague of mine had great difficultly in this area. His business took off like gangbusters for a start up company, and he was on a roll. His ability to sell clients into his program was amazing. He was happy and excited, until it came down to serving the clients. He lost his momentum because there were no clear steps through which to bring the clients. He grew so fast and had no idea how to serve more clients than he had expected. He did not have a solid system. His system was, "I just find clients and serve them." He did not plan for a process, and ultimately his business came to a standstill.

Growth is always an exciting part of your business; however when the growth is happening too fast it is hard to keep up. Managing growth then becomes complex. So how do you keep it simple? You can only do so much, and you can only do what you are talented at doing. Make a list of all your talents and what only you can do. Then make another list of what you don't like to do. Take those two lists and create a job description for yourself (reflecting the role you will assume in your business). With this job description, you will be able to begin to build a system. You must know how you do what you do (the process). You also must find people who are good at the things you struggle with, and then build systems (steps and processes) for what they will do.

In business, you must plan on a daily and consistent basis, so be in the planning stage every day. Remember, an entrepreneur takes action, but also reviews the results of their actions through a system. The system is not only what you do but also how you do it. A system will keep you on track and will also track each client you have and where they are in the process of your services. A good system will guide the client through a great experience.

## Marybeth Hrim's Top Visibility Tip

Gaining visibility is the most important business action for entrepreneurs. How many of you are shy and feel vulnerable? If you said "yes" to feeling vulnerable, you are not alone. Putting yourself out there in the world can be difficult and scary.

Visibility was the most difficult thing for me when I first started my business. Being out in the big world with lots of people . . . yikes! Don't get me wrong. I love talking to people. I love meeting new people and getting to know them and helping them, but putting myself out there was a scary thing. I felt that if I were visible, all my mistakes and shortcomings would rise to the surface and I would be rejected. This is life. We are not perfect, and we all have shortcomings. Rejection is the number one thing people fear most in business. The truth is, if you are going to do business with others, you need to be noticed. So where and how do you start to become visible?

Visibility is a process and should be done with care and honesty. Always be you. Visibility is about responsibility. You owe it to yourself and to others to be a person of good character. My good friend and mentor John Maxwell says, "Charisma will get you in the door, but character will keep you there." This certainly is true on many levels. I believe first impressions are important, but they are not everything. You indeed want to make a good impression, but you also want to be you. If someone is going to do business with you, it will be because you are consistent in who you are, not because of the great impression you gave.

Before you are visible you must have a plan, and you must be responsible for that plan. Your business, life, and reputation depend on it. So how do you actually become visible?

Becoming visible is really quite simple. Technology has made it so. First, you need to embrace social media. If you are not connected to Facebook, Twitter, LinkedIn, or any of the other social sites, start out slowly. Sign up for one. Facebook is a very social site where people are looking for conversations and to build relationships, so begin posting your interests. I am a dog-lover and a golfer. I will post a few days a week about my dog or my golf game (of course depending on how well I played). This helps people connect with you on a much deeper level and get to know what interests you. You will be surprised how many people have the same interests. Facebook and Twitter have made visibility rather simple. However, there are some drawbacks.

The difficulty begins when and if you post negativity, or if you get caught up in arguments over controversial issues. These areas tend to get people fired up, and if they disagree with you online, arguments start and the relationship is tarnished. I have seen people become very brutal if they are passionate about one side or the other on an issue. So be very careful with how you engage in sensitive issues. I personally stay away from those. I don't feel the need to impose my beliefs onto others. I firmly believe that every negative post requires ten or more positive posts to gain back credibility.

Social media is the best way to get to know people and have them get to know the true you. Send someone a nice private note today and stay consistent in how you post. Before long people will not only connect with you, but be on common ground with you. People connect with people they share interests with. Stay connected and be visible.

**Marybeth Hrim's Top Sales Tip**

Some people feel that making sales is one of the most difficult things we have to do our businesses. However, it's mandatory. Without sales and the resulting revenue, you have no business. One of the first things you must do is figure out how long your sales cycle is. For some businesses and industries, the sales cycle is relatively short, and for others it's much longer than we expect. For example, if you are in the restaurant business, your sales cycle will be short, and customers make the purchasing decision before walking in the door. If you are in the personal/professional development and consulting business, your sales cycle could be much longer. Most consulting businesses require you to build relationships, and relationships take time. Patience and persistence are required for persistence through such sales cycles.

Sales are about relationships. The days of the sales person on the street corner screaming, "wanna buy, wanna buy?" are over. Working in the people business, I must always be interested in people and their needs. I remember when I first started my business. I had no idea how I was going to "sell" people into my services. I attended many networking events, and I saw a lot of people that did go around with "wanna buy, wanna buy?" attitudes. I then met a friend and asked him how this networking thing worked, and I never forgot what he said to me that evening. He said, "You want to be interested in your prospect, not interesting." That has stayed with me since. It makes perfect sense. In order to sell, you must know your client. You must be interested in their needs, not your need for selling them.

It takes effort to build relationships, and especially relationships that last. As a business owner, I want to build a community of people. When you build a community of people, you help others in a way unlike any other. You can't do it alone. It takes community to make an impact. So the bottom line is, building not only relationships, but building a community of people will get you further faster. It really does take a village to build a prosperous and thriving business. Sales equal relationships, and relationships equal sales.

## Marybeth Hrim's Top Money Tip

Money certainly helps us live. Without it we are not able to put a roof over our heads, clothes on our backs, and food in our mouths. No doubt about it, we need money in order to survive. However, money is about attitude. It's not how much you have but how you use it. I learned that lesson a long time ago. Don't get me wrong, money is a good thing, but it must be viewed properly in order to do good things with it.

Don't be a hostage to money. Money is a subject that is uncomfortable for people. You either have it or you don't. It really seems like there is no in between. However, in business, you must have an attitude of investment, not just giving or getting, and there is a huge difference.

Most entrepreneurs, when they first begin their businesses, spend money on things they think will "get" them more money, and don't think through what the real return on investment will be. This type of investing or spending will get entrepreneurs in debt very quickly. The advice here is very simple. You must know your numbers. You must know what the return on investment will be and how long it will take to get that return. Is this an investment that needs to be invested in *now,* or can it wait a few months or even a year or so?

Opening a business is much like marrying young with nothing. You must begin with what you have, and build the rest. Get consultation from someone who understands your business and what you need to begin with, and what can wait. Sometimes waiting to invest is the best thing to do. You don't need everything right off the bat, you just need the basics.

I know about making the hard decisions to wait on investing in things I felt I couldn't live without, or things that were tempting because they seemed like exactly what I needed to make a difference.

My best advice on money is to really make thorough choices on what and how to spend money in your business. Spending money in ways that won't drive your business, or that will benefit your business very little, can deplete your resources quickly. It's really so simple, and it's about choices. So choose wisely.

## About Marybeth Hrim

Marybeth Hrim is a Certified Coach with the John Maxwell Team, an international organization committed to developing leaders. She's a teacher and speaker with over 18 years experience helping people achieve their maximum potential.

Marybeth helps companies and individuals cultivate harmony. She believes creating harmony in life, family, and business leads to an abundance of peace.

Marybeth holds a Master's Degree in both Social work and Business Administration with a concentration in Leadership.

## Learn more about Marybeth Hrim at MBHrim.com

# Chapter 12

# ≥Brilliant Tips≤ from Ann Jenrette-Thomas

## Ann Jenrette-Thomas' Top Mindset Tip

### *Redefine Failure*

Failure—eeeww! No one likes to talk about it. No one wants to feel it. So, what do we as business owners do to avoid failing?

*Everything!* We wait to launch our products, or services, or marketing materials, until they are "perfect" so that our endeavor won't fail. We avoid going to certain networking groups or talking to certain people (who we think may reject us), so that we don't feel like a failure. We don't dare to dream big or be audacious in what we ask for, because we don't want to fail.

Avoiding failure wastes time and valuable energy that you need to succeed. So instead, get comfortable with failure.

Redefine failure as a necessary step to success. One of the key reasons why Walt Disney was such a success was because his company embraced failure. In fact, they celebrated it. Your level of success directly correlates with the number of times that you have failed. So, redefine failure as a necessary milestone to get you one step closer to achieving the success that you want. Instead of being afraid of it, accept that it is a normal part of owning a business.

How do you normalize failure? By having a system in place to debrief business actions. A debriefing system can be as simple as asking yourself the following two questions about every business action:

1. "What went well?"

2. "What could we do better next time?"

## Ann Jenrette-Thomas' Top Business Management Tip

### *Set Goals That Work*

One of the key problems I see among business owners is that they waste a lot of time doing things that are not productive. How do you ensure success? Set goals that work. Accomplishing goals is an ever-changing process, not a one shot deal.

Here's a five-step process to help you achieve your goals. First, have a vision for your business. Then schedule time in your calendar to follow each of these steps:

1. One year—Identify the top one to three things you could do in one year that will have the biggest impact in achieving your vision.

2. 90 Days—Break the yearly goals into quarterly milestones (work backwards).

3. Monthly—Break down what *must* be accomplished at the end of each month to meet your 90 day goals.

4. Weekly—Identify what *must* be accomplished at the end of each week to meet your monthly goals.

5. Daily—focus on daily tasks that accomplish your weekly goals. Here's a *bonus tip*: set a time limit for each daily task and then set a timer as you begin each task. When the timer goes off, that's it—move on to the next task (pencil in another time to complete the task if it wasn't finished). After some time, you will train your brain to complete within the time frame.

By using this process, you are destined to achieve your vision. It may seem tedious, but it works!

## Ann Jenrette-Thomas' Top Visibility Tip

### *Leverage Your Content*

Different platforms reach different people within your target market. It's important to get your business on a multitude of platforms. The challenge for most business owners is that they tend to feel overwhelmed, asking themselves, "How am I supposed to create time to write articles, respond to social media, create videos, etc. *and* provide my services or products?" The key is to leverage your content.

Here's How:

> Use client and customer experiences to write an article. Share key insights from client/customer experiences that would benefit your market.

> Find a complementary photo and post the article on your blog. Take advantage of automated social share options including Pinterest.

- Take 15 minutes to pull out short quotes from your article and load them into a social media scheduler (such as Hoot Suite) to preschedule Facebook, Twitter, and LinkedIn posts over the next week. (*Bonus*: hire a graphic artist to convert the quotes into pictures for Facebook and Pinterest).

- Create a video where you discuss the content of the article (if you're camera shy, consider making a short webinar), upload this onto YouTube and share this link on social media too.

- Create an ezine (virtual newsletter) that offers a brief paragraph from your blog articles or videos and includes a link to the full content (again use automated social share links).

See how just ONE client or customer experience can create content that can be shared with your target market in a variety of ways?

## Ann Jenrette-Thomas' Top Sales Tip

### *Rehearse Your Pitch in Front of an Audience*

You know your business inside and out. You know how your product or service helps your clients/customers. The problem is that you are too intimately involved with your product or service. Things that seem obvious to you may actually feel confusing to your prospects. As the old adage goes, "Confused people don't buy."

If you want to increase sales, then you have to realize that it's not enough to have an awesome product or service. You have to talk about it in a way that is crystal clear to your prospect, and compels them to buy. This takes practice.

First, write out your sales pitch (you shouldn't wing it). The pitch should specifically address how your service or product helps your prospect. When talking about price, demonstrate the true value of the product/service to your prospect. Think about any incentives you want to offer to encourage fast action. Finally, include testimonials of satisfied customers/clients.

Now, practice your pitch. Practice at least three times on your own. Then, practice in front of others who will give you honest feedback. At the end of your rehearsal, ask the audience the following questions:

1. What am I selling?

2. Did any part confuse you?

3. Did any part make you feel uncomfortable?

4. Would you want to buy?

5. What could I do better?

Modify your pitch some more based on the feedback and practice, before meeting with your prospects. You'll feel more confident and close more deals.

## Ann Jenrette-Thomas' Top Money Tip

### *Ten Questions to Make Your Money Grow*

One of the biggest mistakes I made in my early years of business was that I didn't track any of my numbers. Then I listened to a talk by sales coach, Julie Steelman, where she discussed the importance of tracking your sales. To do so, ask yourself the following ten questions at the end of the month to help you grow your business:

1. What did I plan to sell?

2. What did I actually sell?

3. Did I notice any trends?

4. Was I above or below my monthly goal?

5. If below, what happened?

   a. Do I need to do more of something or less of something in the next month?

   b. What change could I make so I can exceed next month's goal and make up for the dip?

   c. How could I make next month more profitable?

6. If above, what contributed to increased success this month?

   a. How could I repeat that next month?

   b. How could I use the momentum from this month to increase sales in a low month?

   c. What am I going to do to celebrate this positive outcome?

7. Do I want to change anything so that things are easier in the future?

8. What did I learn that I could use to my advantage later?

9. How am I feeling about my plan?

10. Do I need to tweak it or revamp it?

Tracking these answers will help you be more profitable.

## About Ann Jenrette-Thomas

Ann Jenrette-Thomas, Esq., CPCC, is an attorney, professional certified coach, and author. Ann has spent nearly 18 years helping business owners overcome obstacles to success. Ann calls upon her rich experience, coupled with her extensive training and knowledge in organizational development and coaching, to provide her clients with effective solutions that balance both the underlying needs of the business to remain viable, as well as individual needs of the business owner to feel balanced.

**Learn more about Ann Jenrette-Thomas at EsquireCoaching.com**

# Chapter 13

# ≳Brilliant Tips≲ from Lisa Mohl Kaplin

## Lisa Mohl Kaplin's Top Mindset Tip

The most important aspect of success in business is related to the mindset of the business owner. What you think leads directly to how you feel, and that affects how you behave. If you are in a constant state of worry about your business (about how much money you don't have, what might go wrong, or whether or not your employees are producing, for example), you are likely to feel rather weighted down and miserable.

If that's how you feel, it is nearly impossible for you to make appropriate, creative, and well thought out decisions about your business.

So how do you change this? First, you must identify the underlying belief system about yourself and your business. Do you think you are doomed to failure, not a risk taker, or not creative enough? Do you worry that you are in the wrong business at the wrong time? Check those belief systems and see if they are actually accurate. Next, if they aren't accurate, you need to change them. This is often easier said than done because our brain is programmed to believe what we've been telling it for years. You need to reprogram that brain to believe something different.

Start laying out new belief systems for yourself and then repeat them constantly, almost like a mantra. Some examples might be, "I'm creative and talented." "I'm good at making money." "Money comes easily and effortlessly to me." Think of some mindset changes that are positive and forward thinking that make sense to you. Start saying them and you will change not only your mindset but also the trajectory of your business.

It's also important to surround yourself with people who have similar mindsets about your business. This doesn't necessarily mean people who always agree with you but rather people who believe in the concept and greater good of your company.

## Lisa Mohl Kaplin's Top Business Management Tip

Let's talk productivity and why we often get stuck and become less productive than we'd like. The best thing to do when you aren't productive is to sit down, take a few deep breaths, and figure out what is keeping you stuck. We are often unproductive when we are overwhelmed, fearful for some reason, or unclear on what needs to be done. Figure out if it is overwhelm, fear, or lack of clarity. You will then be in a better position to make the needed changes to get back to peak productivity.

If you are overwhelmed, figure out what exactly needs to be done, how you want to prioritize it, and if it's possible to delegate some of it to someone else. Entrepreneurs can often be very detail-oriented and a tad bit controlling. If you want to be productive, delegate tasks that aren't your strength, and stick to the things that you do best. If after some analysis, you realize that you are fearful or anxious of an upcoming task or event, try to figure out why this might be. Is it a lack of knowledge, concern of the unknown, or maybe an irrational fear? Once you understand the fear, you have a better chance of conquering it.

Finally, are you stuck due to a lack of clarity on what needs to be done? Whenever I find that I keep putting the same task on my calendar day after day, I know that it's either something that really doesn't need to be done or something about which I am not clear. If it's a clarity issue, break the task or event into smaller pieces and then design a plan for each component. Procrastination is rarely laziness or a lack of motivation. There is almost always an underlying cause. If you figure out the cause, you'll find that you are productive and purposeful.

## Lisa Mohl Kaplin's Top Visibility Tip

Blog, blog, blog! Many entrepreneurs shy away from blogging, either due to worry about their writing skills, or from the concern that it will take too much of their time. Yet a blog is the simplest, most inexpensive way to get the word out about you and your company. Many people read blogs as news or business articles, and why shouldn't yours be available to those people?

If you aren't a great writer, consider contracting someone to write content for you (that you can approve), or hiring a virtual assistant who can write. Your blog should do a few important things. First, use the blog to allow people to know, trust, and like you. Share some of yourself in the blog, such as your mistakes, your struggles, or your victim to victory story. This will allow your readers to know that you are like them, and it will allow them to trust and like you.

Your blog should also be used to educate your reader, to entertain your reader, and to show your reader that you are an expert in your field. Share stories about clients you've helped, without sounding too "salesy" or pushy. Write a blog about a typical problem that potential clients may face, and then show them why you are an expert, and how your expertise may help them. Make sure to entertain as well, with humorous antidotes, inspirational stories, or appropriate jokes.

Blogging is easy to do. Blog either for your website or for an online newspaper or magazine. Blog about three to four times a month, and then share it with your list and on social media. This is the quickest, cheapest, and easiest way to get visible fast, raise your SEO, and build credibility.

## Lisa Mohl Kaplin's Top Sales Tip

This may sound obvious, but I'm often amazed at how many business owners miss this; completely believe in your product and why the people you will be selling to will benefit from it. Believe that you will be doing them a disservice if you do not offer them your product or service (since not offering it would keep them from solving their problem or concern).

If you don't currently believe in yourself, your company, or your products, you need to address that before you even consider a sales plan. When you don't believe in yourself, neither will anyone else.

Once you firmly have in your mind how your product can truly serve someone, your sales pitch won't be a "sale" but rather a conversation in which you share something that will greatly benefit your potential client. Your words will convey your belief system in a genuine and caring way. I know without question, that when a woman works with me, together we will change her life for the better. When I'm telling a potential client about myself and my services, my belief in how I can serve them shines through, without some choreographed sales pitch.

Think about what keeps your future clients up at night, what worries them? Do you have a product or service that will help them change that worry? If so, tell them exactly how it will serve them and how their life will change because of it. Don't describe the product in too much detail but rather describe the change in their life that will come, once they have your product or service. What will change in their lives after they work with you? Tell them what that is and watch your sales soar.

## Lisa Mohl Kaplin's Top Money Tip

My top money tip is a prosperity plan. Most of the business owners that I talk to, have quite a few negative and fearful thoughts around money. This is probably one of the easiest ways to guarantee *future* struggles with money. A prosperity plan is one in which you identify your money mindset, see if it is a helpful one, and if not, change it.

First, think carefully about what you say to yourself about money. Do you say, "I never have enough money." or "Money never comes easily to me." or even worse, "Money is evil and I'm working for the greater good, not for money."

It's important to change your money mindset to one in which you believe that what you are selling is worth someone paying you well for it. Money is a good thing if used in a healthy and conscious manner, and we need not fear a lack of money, since that will not give us the emotional energy we need to go out and run a profitable business. A prosperity plan is one in which you change your mindset and outlook on money so that you are open to earning more, and spending in a reliable and appropriate way to build your business.

I strongly recommend you use affirmations within your prosperity plan. Most of us have very negative messages about money that pervade our thoughts. Prosperity affirmations will help you change these negative messages and open you to opportunities that will allow you to be prosperous. When we have negative money thoughts, we often miss quality opportunities to grow our business and our profits. Some prosperity examples might be, "Money comes easily and effortlessly to me," or "Money allows me to live a full and exciting life," and "People pay me well for a service that is very beneficial to them." Say these affirmations frequently, particularly when you start feeling stress or anxiety about money.

## About Lisa Mohl Kaplin

Dr. Lisa Kaplin has a master's degree and doctorate in psychology. She is also a certified professional life coach. Lisa's company, Smart Women Inspired Lives, helps women who feel stuck in their personal or professional lives find their voice and reach their highest potential.

Lisa is also a corporate trainer for American Management Association, Aetna, Kraft, and others focusing on psychologically related topics such as communication, stress management, and women's assertiveness.

**Learn more about Lisa Mohl Kaplin at SmartWomenInspiredLives.com**

# Chapter 14

# ≥Brilliant Tips≤ from Kathi C. Laughman

## Kathi C. Laughman's Top Mindset Tip

Mindset is not about our thoughts. It is about our beliefs. Our mindset works like a thermostat for our life (and business). Our "mind" "sets" at a specific point defined by a belief. It might be hot, cold, or anywhere in between. We "can," we "can't," or "maybe." What happens next? Anything and everything we do is going to be countered (and influenced) by that set point. So no matter what happens, actions will be triggered to make everything stay true to the set point, just like a thermostat. The response is involuntary. Whatever has to happen to bring everything back to that "set point" (mindset) will happen. What is remarkable about this is that all it takes to change the outcome is to adjust the set point. Reset your thermostat. Change your belief (mindset) and you can and will change your results.

Here is the best way to change your mindset: give your "mind" something that requires a response that serves your outcome. Ask yourself a question. Instead of just saying affirmations as declarations (which, by the way, the mind truly can ignore), use questions to force the recognition of true belief. In other words, check your "temperature" setting. Your mind cannot ignore a question.

For example, if you want to reach a goal by a certain date, instead of just saying you will, turn it first into a question. "Can I reach this goal by this date?" If your answer isn't *yes*, you need to adjust the thermostat! Get to your own *yes* first, and everything else will follow.

## Kathi C. Laughman's Top Business Management Tip

Whether you are running a home-based business or a global enterprise, many of the same principals are going to apply. One of those principals is that in every business, there are only three or four activities that actually drive the majority of your business results. Everything else is ancillary to those main things. It is essential that you know what those are for your business and that you measure and monitor those activities every single day.

These are your *Key Performance Indicators* or KPI's. These can change over time as your business develops and grows, but there will always be three of four measurements that should guide your decisions and your actions. One of them may be about bringing prospects into your company. Another should focus on the conversion of prospects to customers. Next is a measurement that is focused on a key element in service delivery. And the final should zero in on repeat customer business or some aspect of customer loyalty. Determine a key activity that contributes in each of these areas and have a way to see information about them every day. You should know these numbers inside and out, and be highly sensitive and responsive to changes (up or down).

For example, you should monitor and know what your average percentage rate is for converting prospects to customers. That indicator will tell you how many prospects you are reaching in order to grow your customer base. If you aren't hitting your prospect number every day, you also won't hit your customer number (sales) that month.

A relentless focus on these key activities will drive your business forward and keep you from being distracted by details that will not materially impact your results. Focus on what matters.

## Kathi C. Laughman's Top Visibility Tip

One channel for visibility that is often ignored by smaller home based companies is cause-based marketing and partnering. There are studies that show that over 55 percent of the American buying public has and will purchase products or services from a company primarily because of causes that it promotes and supports. Think about that. When you align with a particular cause, not only are you doing your part to give back to your community, you are also positioning yourself for greater business visibility. You will attract ready to buy prospects based on your values first, and your products or services second.

It is important to make a distinction between national and local causes. For the smaller business, a local cause will create a stronger profile. It creates a win-win-win scenario. They win, you win and your customers win. Everyone can feel satisfaction from the transaction and the relationship.

Another important point is that cause marketing and partnering is not about donating money. It is about actual partnering. This means ad placements on their websites and links from your website back to theirs. It means special products designed to drive contributions to them. It can mean sponsoring or co-sponsoring events with them. And quite often, it means being afforded the opportunity to access and speak with their other contributors, volunteers, and supporters.

This approach to market visibility will bring with it free public relations and media exposure. Developed wisely, the partnership can deliver a return for both you and the cause you support.

## Kathi C. Laughman's Top Sales Tip

When we prepare for a sales conversation, we often focus solely on being certain that we know how to adequately describe our product or service and its value. We focus the preparation on what we are going to say first. The reality is that it is what we say second that is really going to make the difference. Because in most cases, the first response we get is going to be an objection or an attempt to divert our attention away from selling. Why? Because while we all love to buy; none of us likes to be sold.

That means that we should focus our preparation as much (if not more) on how we can counter their concerns and objections deftly in ways that create a comfortable conversation. There are only four primary types of objections:

1. Not convinced of need

2. Lack of money

3. Time or timing

4. Not convinced we are the best option

Therefore, that is where you must focus—beyond your own enthusiasm—for the value of what you do.

One of the best responses I've come across in a long time, relates to a combination of both time and money. Here was the response: "I completely understand. Things are tight right now, but something I've learned is that my financial situation today is almost always the result of a decision I made six months ago. What is going to be different for you in six months if you don't do something different now?" Guess what? I found the money and invested!

## Kathi C. Laughman's Top Money Tip

When it comes to our money, we have to be equally concerned about how it is being spent as we are with how it is being generated. As business owners, we have to understand our top line, our bottom line, and every line in between. When we understand cost, we make better decisions on everything.

For example, if you know that your average ad cost per sale to bring on a customer is $5 and you run a campaign that allows you to hit a $3 mark, you know that you are going to want to study that campaign to determine how you were able to achieve that reduction in cost, so you can repeat it. If you didn't know your average before was $5, you might mistakenly think that $3 was too high and even decline the opportunity.

The key cost numbers you should know at a minimum are your break-even point, your cost to gain a customer, and the cost to produce each of your products/services. The cost considerations beyond these that you need to know, are "buy vs. own" and opportunity cost.

Buy vs. own is essential for the home-based solopreneur, because this will help guide decisions about outsourcing. What is the cost to outsource something vs. producing it internally? The same is true for opportunity cost. Quite often we are dealing with limited resources, so whatever we decide to "spend" on something is in fact going to mean that we won't be able to do something else. It's important to factor that into your decision process. Is the return on the new investment superior to what you are already getting? If not, the opportunity cost isn't worth the change in your spending.

## About Kathi C. Laughman

Kathi Laughman is a strategist, speaker, and author. In 2008 she founded The Mackenzie Circle, a life coaching and personal leadership company, in order to work with entrepreneurs as their possibility partner, coach, and mentor.

Kathi also works with non-profit organizations focused on education and women's issues. She is certified (CPC) by the International Coaching Federation and by the Institute for Professional Excellence in Coaching as a master practitioner (ELI-MP).

## Learn more about Kathi C. Laughman at MackenzieCircle.com

# Chapter 15

# ≥Brilliant Tips≤ from Blaze Lazarony

## Blaze Lazarony's Top Mindset Tip

A wise and wonderful businesswoman once shared this insight with me, "Everything you need is right there on the tip of your nose!"

She is absolutely correct; it's there, out of range of your immediate eyesight. How do you see what's there? You ask for help!

Many of my entrepreneurial clients come to me exhausted and burned out, clinging to the belief that they have to figure out and do everything themselves. They don't, and neither do you!

So how do you start? First, you call a truce with that part of you that still believes your business is all about the act of *you* doing everything. Next, you embrace the reality that successful business owners ask for help, support, and guidance.

When you seek and receive help, your challenges get easier, and answers appear that were seemingly invisible before. I believe that being in business is a spiritual journey, and many times we simply need the loving support of another to carry us through both the joyous and difficult times. That's why I encourage entrepreneurs to have at least one coach or mentor in their lives, because the truth is, we're not meant to travel this path alone.

When you begin to trust in another human being, and surrender to the fears that can accompany asking for help, you'll find that more of life becomes possible.

So ask yourself: is there something in your business life that seems challenging right now? Who do you know that could help you ease the burden that you're facing? Allow the first ideas to surface. Then reach out and ask for support.

As you look to others for answers and guidance, I trust that you'll begin to find that more of what you wanted and needed has actually been there all along, right there—on the tip of our nose.

## Blaze Lazarony's Top Business Management Tip

Every entrepreneur I know is constantly doing numerous tasks each week: juggling clients, business development, marketing, and so much more—in addition to fulfilling personal responsibilities.

When I worked in the corporate world, I managed my weekly calendar by setting goals. As an entrepreneur I set intentions instead. For me, goals felt too much like a to-do list; they can help us guide our energies, but they also can lead us to feeling constrained by an endless list of should-dos. Have you ever had a should-do on your list and not completed it? It felt disappointing, right?

With intentions on the other hand, the whole process feels lighter, more holistic, and fluid. By using intentions, you can begin to feel less constrained to achieve each milestone by a specific date, and become more invested into achieving each outcome in a well-rounded way, and with more ease and flexibility.

Years ago, a business mentor of mine shared this tip: you overestimate what you can do in a day, week or even a month; and underestimate what you can achieve in six months or year!

It's true, we fill our daily and weekly calendars to the brim with tasks that we typically can't get completed in two weeks, and when we plan longer range tasks, we can actually accomplish more than we think we can.

So, are you ready to take the challenge? Write down your intentions for the next year; these are the high level accomplishments that you'd like to achieve one year from now. Then take that list and divide it into two six-month periods. Next, break each of those lists into monthly intentions. Finally, separate the monthly items into weekly intentions.

If you're like many of my clients who begin this practice, you'll actually find yourself achieving many of your yearlong intentions at the six to eleven month mark, with ease and flexibility. How cool is that? I encourage you to try it for yourself!

## Blaze Lazarony's Top Visibility Tip

*You* are the light of your business!

You become a 24/7 walking and breathing billboard for your brand, because your business and your brand are merely extensions of you.

When you design your brand, do it with intention, and make a commitment to discovering your essence, or what I also call, your "inner spark", first and foremost. Attempting to create your brand without knowing your inner spark is like trying to start a fire with just crumbled up bits of newspaper and a small pile of logs, without a fuel source. It's impossible. When you add *you* to the process, you literally become the fuel—the inner spark—that has the potential to grow into a fire that can eventually light up the entire world.

Discovering your inner spark takes time; it's about connecting to the truth of who you are at the soul level, so you can then logically and emotionally communicate your inner spark to others. One way to do this is to use positive words, symbols, and even colors that share your brand with your clients in an easy to understand and relatable method.

Next, you literally embody your brand and it becomes a reflection of you. Quite frankly, we're always doing this, we simply may not be consciously aware of it. The invitation is for you to be authentic and transparent as you create your brand, and then show up everywhere, both in person and online, being in alignment with your brand and sharing your unique and radiant inner spark! Simply watch your visibility grow as you embrace and embody your inner spark. You'll be amazed at the transformation.

Need help finding your inner spark? Read Chapter two in *The Art & Science of Loving Yourself First: 'cause your business should complete you, not deplete you!* (Splendor Publishing, 2013)

## Blaze Lazarony's Top Sales Tip

Did you know that every single sales transaction could be defined in one easy sentence? It's the act of two parties exchanging one valuable good or service, for money or its energy equivalent, including other goods or services.

As an entrepreneur, you most likely focus on optimizing the product or service that you offer to others. Therefore, if you sell an item, you want it to be the highest quality product that will yield the best payment. Or if you sell a service, you want it to offer your client the easiest solution to their current challenges.

If you follow this business model, your goal is to offer the best quality service or product, at the right time, and for the best price.

I strongly believe there is a critical component to the selling equation that is often overlooked, which I refer to as: life is all relationships, make them matter!

Yes, it's actually the relationships that are the secret to sales success!

For 20 years, I worked in a high level executive role in the fast-paced retail industry. This world became my living and breathing business think-tank, because I had the chance to put so many different business strategies and plans into practice. And what I realized was, it was actually the individual players, the people intimately involved in the transaction itself, who ultimately made the sale happen or not. And a critical component of each of these business transactions was actually the quality of relationship that these two people had together.

Think about your own business and ask yourself: how are my relationships with clients? How much does each relationship matter to me? And what could I do or say to improve my business relationships?

This single tip can be the ultimate game changer for your business. So the next time you choose to create a new good or service, or improve a current one, also think about how you can optimize that unique relationship with each and every client. Because when you understand that each relationship is actually worth more than the sales transaction itself, your bottom-line profits will be overflowing!

## Blaze Lazarony's Top Money Tip

I believe money is a simple form of energy—just like heat, water, electricity, and even our physical life force. And as with every form, it's all about finding a delicate balance of the flow of energy; it's not a static balance, rather a dynamic and ever moving balance.

For example, plants need water to grow and thrive. Add too much water and the plant will drown, or deprive it of water and it will wither and die. Each plant needs a dynamic balance of the right amount of water, at the right time in its growing cycle, to grow into the healthiest plant possible.

So lean in close, I have a question for you: how do you feel about the current flow of energy into your business? Does it feel like a steady in-stream of ideas, clients, and cash? Or is it a trickle, which seems to have spits and starts?

I believe your flow of energy, especially as it relates to money, is directly proportional to your internal energetic state.

If you are in alignment with abundance consciousness, you will physically experience abundance, because you will attract people to your bright and radiant energy. Would you rather purchase something from an authentic, positive, and smiling person or from someone who is conflicted, frustrated, and angry? It's exactly the same for your clients.

Check in with yourself and ask how you can improve your money energy flow. It all begins with an internal shift of your energy to a higher vibration and dynamic balance—embracing states such as awareness, love, abundance, joy, and happiness. People, money, and viewpoints will become more positive and possible when you are living in this state of energetic flow.

For many of my clients, they can shift into a higher flow of energy simply by getting in touch with their inner spark, those core qualities of who they are at the heart and soul level as described in words, colors, or symbols. And as they live more from their inner spark, they become a magnet for other people and situations that match their internal energetic vibration. I invite you to try on a more positive money energy for yourself.

## About Blaze Lazarony

Blaze Lazarony is an Entrepreneurial Business Strategist, Founder of the Entrepreneur Networking Collective, Author, and Speaker. For 20 years Blaze held high-level positions at a Fortune 100 company, delivering outstanding customer service, and driving bottom line profits. Today, her passion is helping high-achieving women create soul-based lives, and custom fit businesses that light up the world with their unique brilliance.

**Learn more about Blaze Lazarony at BlazeABrilliantPath.com**

# Chapter 16

# ≷Brilliant Tips≷ from Diana Matteson-Oliveira

## Diana Matteson-Oliveira's Top Mindset Tip

### *Stay in the Present and Surrender to the Outcome*

What is real is what is happening now, this very minute. If you are not present, not in the now, in mind and in body, you are not at your best. You are not operating at your optimum. If you're running a hundred miles an hour trying to multitask in order to get everything done, you won't really accomplish much, certainly nothing worthwhile. You're too exhausted and overwhelmed to even think, much less be creative.

We are human beings, not human doings. As a single mom, I've become a master at multitasking. I've been chronically overextended and overcommitted, putting so much pressure on myself to be the best at everything. It's impossible. I found out that the quest to be the best, and thinking I could control everything to make that possible, became an emotional straightjacket. I couldn't breathe. I couldn't see. I was exhausted, hindering my efforts and myself.

I learned that what I think, might not be what I need. We need to learn to be still and ask the universe for guidance, and trust the outcome without forcing the results we desire. There is a time to act and a time to let go and surrender. We can be "our best" by surrendering control and allowing the process of our lives to unfold naturally.

Using this mindset, I've been very successful, as have the multitude of clients I've mentored. It's a skill that takes focus and discipline. It's hard to break old habits, especially our thinking and the habitual thoughts running through our minds. If we can learn to still those thoughts, be present in the moment, and stop the noise, we will be much more creative, more imaginative, and far more productive. Success will come.

## Diana Matteson-Oliveira's Top Business Management Tip

### *Build a Team that Resonates with Your Style and Vision*

As an entrepreneur, there is a fine line between success and failure. Today, it is critical that we do not squander our opportunities by spreading ourselves too thin. I have learned that success in business can only be achieved if you have steady growth, while investing in a team that grows with you. They must be capable of executing their roles at the highest level, and they must resonate with your style and vision.

Surround yourself with gifted professionals. Learn to recognize originality and talent, and try to have these people on your team. Discover what you do best, and build your team with those who are skilled in the areas that you are not.

For example, I have a client who is a brilliant designer. She found that in order to keep work flowing in, she had to do the sales, marketing, finances, design, and project management herself. This was so overwhelming that she could no longer do quality work that her clients expected. Together, we crafted a collaborative team to work with her, freeing her to focus on the clients design needs and expectations. Hiring a part-time bookkeeper for the invoicing kept the cash flow current. Now the money flows in and the bills are paid, while she gets to focus on what she's great at doing.

Think of the "three legged stool" concept. Each leg is needed to keep the stool upright. The same is true for a business. The three essential elements are:

1. Your expertise (product or service)

2. Marketing and sales

3. Financial management

As an entrepreneur or professional, we bring to the "stool" our own skill set that must be augmented by other resources in order to grow and be successful.

## Diana Matteson-Oliveira's Top Visibility Tip

### *The Goal is Longevity—Not to be a One-Hit-Wonder!*

Are you a one-hit-wonder? Take your time creating your brand, and make it memorable. You want your image, your reputation, and your brand to be recognized and to stand the test of time.

Statistics show that exposure to a product or services at least seven times will lead to more sales. What keeps prospective clients interested in your brand? It would be something you offer that is unique, something with quality, and something with a superb image. It is what reflects *your* personal and professional style. This is the image and branding you want to present to the world. I see far too many cookie cutter brands with "me too" marketing that won't endure over time. Set yourself apart.

No matter what business you're in, all the products, programs, videos, graphics, and websites must be masterfully crafted to distinguish you and your personal brand. What is your image? How do you want to be perceived? Make the investment and effort to figure it out in order to stand out and be successful.

We know what Apple, Facebook and Starbucks images are. Their brands are brilliantly engineered into their entire business architecture. Give some serious thought to your branding and image of your company when deciding what you want to be known for.

You must be very selective in the design of your collateral materials and website. They must reflect your style, your vision, and your values. They must invite pursuit; create curiosity, and the desire to work with you or your company. Create an image that reflects you and connects you with your prospective audience. Be outstanding. There are no shortcuts here. This is your time to shine.

## Diana Matteson-Oliveira's Top Sales Tip

### *Discover Your Personal Style*

After more than three decades in sales, and having mastered many techniques designed to sell to my target market and close the deal, I've come to realize how authenticity in presenting yourself and your product or service is the key to success.

I learned this the hard way. My first sales presentation was the introduction of the "personal computer." I learned as much as I could about the technical features, but I was still overwhelmed with anxiety about how I would be perceived, and I ended up running to the women's bathroom in tears.

Determined to overcome this humiliation, I threw myself into learning everything I could about sales. I studied every guru and trainer, but all I learned was how to copy what others did, which resulted in my presentations feeling scripted, phony, and disingenuous. I wasn't being "me."

So I set out to find my true authentic personal sales and presentation style. I relaxed and realized that I could relate authentically and connect with just about anyone. I was no longer attached to the outcome, intimidated by the "sales" process, or afraid to go after any new business opportunities worrying I would be judged on my performance. The results were beyond my expectations.

Let go of your fear of the sales process. Become completely present, be yourself, ask probing questions, then listen to what your prospects want and need. Then, once you have established a connection, you will naturally know when to present your products or services and close the sale. That's it!

The foundation of who you are and how you present yourself is the key to your success. Be *authentic*, be *yourself*, and be *real*. Your success will follow.

## Diana Matteson-Oliveira's Top Money Tip

### *Create Value Beyond Your Price*

Value has more credibility than price. Value is the foundation of developing a lasting quality relationship with your client. It's the sum of all your offerings, experience, and all the trust previous clients have placed in you. It's your reputation.

When you engage with your next new prospect, take the time to get to know them before you try to sell yourself or what you offer. Be in inquiry mode. Really listen, probe, and learn from what they are telling you. Find out what they need and want. They will tell you, if you listen. Once you are clear of their wants and needs, position your product or service to reveal the potential value to them. Once they know you listened and cared, the price becomes irrelevant. Your reputation and the relationship are dependent on the solutions you present with your products or services, specific to their problems or needs. They will feel you are taking care of them.

When they trust in you to deliver what they need, your product or service must be positioned to resolve their specific problem. It is then critical to deliver more than promised. This strategy creates value, which will sustain your relationship far after the sale when you exceed their expectations. The result will be the realization of more referrals and a long-term happy client.

The truth is, when they realize the value in what you offer, they will be more than happy to pay the price.

If there is one thing I have learned from my multi-million dollar sales career as a professional and as an entrepreneur, is that sales is easy. Creating value for the client is what creates the long-term success of your business.

## About Diana Matteson-Oliveira

Diana Matteson-Oliveira is the founder of My Forte' International. As a trusted mentor, she has inspired and empowered entrepreneurial and corporate clients to overcome obstacles, design their vision, and develop powerful skills that achieve results. In over 30 years of sales and marketing, she has manifested millions in revenue as an entrepreneur and corporate professional.

Diana's creative and introspective approach catapults her clients to realize their hidden potential and strategic advantage in their marketplace.

**Learn more about Diana Matteson-Oliveira at MyForteInternational.com**

# Chapter 17

# ≥Brilliant Tips≤ from Kat Mikic

## Kat Mikic's Top Mindset Tip

It all starts in our minds. What we think ultimately creates our reality. If you believe it will be hard, tough, or unfulfilling, it will be, and it will keep showing up in your life in all different areas in many different ways. How you *feel* right now is a direct indication of what you are thinking.

Realistically, we are faced with everyday frustrations and things not always going right in our business. It's bound to happen, and while we do not always have control over all of the events in our lives, we get to *choose* how we *feel* about them and how it will affect us.

Mindset makes the difference between success and failure, and I strongly believe we must consistently be on top of it.

No one is perfect. Even I find myself going off path at times, having to bring myself back to center so I can realign and recollect my thoughts.

We have a lifetime of conditioning on our minds. Just "thinking positive" all the time is not enough—but it does help.

Here are my favorite tools to remain in a positive mindset and keep on the path to getting what I want:

1. Vision board

Create a vision board showing how you want your life to look. I usually just surf the net and look for houses, cars, and pictures that represent how I want to feel and what I want in my life.

2. Power statements

We created a program that shows how to do these. In a nutshell, power statements are positive affirmations on steroids. Positive affirmations on their own will never be enough. To scramble an old thought or pattern we also need to change our physical state of being while reciting the affirmation. The other key to this is stating the affirmation as if it has already happened, such as "I am strong, I am capable, and I have everything I need right now." The most common mistake people make when reciting affirmations is to say them like they "want" it. You need to say it like you already have it. If you focus on the "not having" what you want, you will continue to not have it.

3. Gratitude

Practice daily gratitude and giving thanks for all that you have right now. When you are happy with where you are, it will raise your energetic vibration to allow you to attract more of what you want into your life.

## Kat Mikic's Top Business Management Tip

I am a free spirit. Generally speaking, I am not a systematized person. This has reined havoc on my business from time to time. The best thing I ever did was sign up to a project management system called "Basecamp."

It allows me to keep all of my projects organized and includes task lists, file uploads, notes, and a discussion thread.

I can invite contractors and coaches to my projects, and clients to their own projects. It saves so much mental space and helps me keep it all together.

I like to end one day by planning the next. I still prefer pen and paper—call me old school—but there's just something incredibly satisfying about physically drawing a line through completed tasks. I will go to my Basecamp and pick my top five things for completion, and a few more that aren't urgent. I choose five things for my business and five for client projects, this way I consistently work *on* my business as well as *in* my business. For many of my clients, striking a balance of working in and on the business can be difficult. Specifically creating tasks to help your business evolve is a great way to get around this.

## Kat Mikic's Top Visibility Tip

It is easy to feel that you're in a sea of competition and that you're just lost in the noise among a million other business owners.

My greatest visibility tip is to inter-connect your personal Facebook profile and your business page. I actually get more business from my personal profile, and I really just have my business page there for increased exposure.

The number one thing you *must* do on Facebook is to link your personal profile to your business page. In the "about" section on your personal Facebook profile, you can choose to list where you "work." You can link to your business page there. Make sure your job description says something about what you do if your page name is not so descriptive. For example, mine reads "Online Launch Queen at KatMikic," and when someone clicks on Kat Mikic, they are taken straight to my business page.

When you comment on threads, or post comments to the Facebook section on blogs, this is displayed. It will help you get more traffic back to your business page.

Also on your business page, ensure that the very first line of your description is a hyperlink back to your website. This way it is obvious to a viewer, and they will be more likely to click on it and visit your website.

## Kat Mikic's Top Sales Tip

Many people think "sales" and have fear come up. Marketing and sales have become dirty words, and more often than not, my clients have real blocks around actually taking the money.

If you approach sales from a space of love and service, it completely changes the game. Many years ago, one of my mentors told me "Kat, if *you* don't help them, they will keep looking until they find someone who will, and they will make the sale, not you." This piece of advice changed everything for me.

Consider every single page you have online—whether it is a web page, a download page, a Facebook page, a Pinterest board, a YouTube channel, or a LinkedIn account—as your "web-estate."

Every single one of these pages is an opportunity for you to put out a call to action, either back to one of your services or products, or to a special offering (you just need to be savvy about it).

If you are going to be spending money on advertising, you need to make sure that your sales funnel is ready; otherwise it is just dead money.

You have two options online. You can either lead people directly to a product on a sales page, or lead them to a lead capture page where you capture their details (their name and email address, for example) and offer something of value for free before making a money offer.

Both can work well. If you are going to do lead capture first, and then make offers through a newsletter or your website, I would suggest placing your next offer right on the page where the visitor will come to collect their free gift. This is often overlooked and can be a gold mine.

## Kat Mikic's Top Money Tip

Many of the clients I have worked with over the years (myself included), have hit money blocks. I believe that many of our money issues stem from subconscious beliefs and conditioning created over the entire course of our lives.

It's particularly common to see people undercharging and struggling to incrcase their prices, especially in the startup phase. Many of the women I have worked with have eventually connected this to a lack of "self worth," which was definitely an issue for me at one point.

Sometimes, when our gifts and talents are so natural and things feel "easy" for us, we can seriously underestimate the value of what we are providing. The best way to know whether this is happening is to take a look at your current financial situation. Are you forever running out of money, or is there always more than enough?

If you are on a hamster wheel of having and then not having money, you need to step back from your business and take an objective look at your income and expenses.

Are you tracking expenses? Do you know exactly how much it costs you to operate your business and live? If not, write out everything. Include health care, dental, personal expenses, insurance, taxes, marketing, operational costs, food, fuel, phone, Internet . . . *everything*! Then take a proper look at your income.

How much are you earning on average? How long is it taking you to earn that money, and how much time is it taking from your life?

Divide your income by the amount of hours you work. Look at the *real cost* of being in business.

This can be a real eye opener. At one point, when I calculated the actual *real* sums, I discovered I was earning very little. It was completely unsustainable. I was working myself to death just to get by. It was the reality check I needed to make a change.

I hired people to do the things I didn't want to do. This was a massive step out of my comfort zone, because I didn't want to spend money unnecessarily. Once I made this break, though, it freed me up to reduce my hours worked. I accomplished more in the hours I did work. I was no longer bogged down in tasks I didn't like. In addition, there was more time for me to promote my business. I also increased my fees.

This is a fickle game. To keep moving forward, stay in check. It's easy to get lost in our businesses and delude ourselves into thinking we are doing better than we actually are. At the end of the day, it's black and white, facts and figures. Either you're making money or you're not. Either your business is providing you the lifestyle you want, or it's consuming you. If you have fear in this area, now is the perfect time to step in and step up.

## About Kat Mikic

Kat Mikic is passionate about helping women launch and grow a thriving online profile and business. She is the founder of KatMikic.com which is all about "Creating the Freedom

Lifestyle." Kat's mission is to help you become a woman of influence and the "go to" person in your niche, so that you can create alternate income streams that are not reliant on you always having to be in your business.

**Learn more about Kat Mikic at KatMikic.com**

# Chapter 18

## ≥Brilliant Tips≤ from Kimberly Pitts

### Kimberly Pitts' Top Mindset Tip

I often see firsthand how entrepreneurs consciously and unconsciously hinder themselves by allowing fear, reluctance, and self doubt to keep them from really investing in themselves and in their businesses. Your "triggers" pop up at the moment when you need to grow and step out.

Typically entrepreneurs experience fear, reluctance and self-doubt in situations like these:

≥ When it is time to make a decision in your business that will propel it to a new level

≥ When the decision looks similar to a situation or program you tried before that did not work, or that ended badly

≥ When the decision requires a certain level of time and financial commitment from you

So what do you do to press forward?

### *Make Wise and Consistent Decisions*

The most successful entrepreneurs tend to make wise decisions. Weigh the pros and cons of any decision you need to make to move your business forward, and filter whether you are allowing any fears, self-doubt, or reluctance to guide your decisions.

### *Feel the Fear and Do It Anyway*

I don't know any entrepreneur that has never felt some level of fear. It is natural. Refuse to sit on the sidelines of your life, and don't allow what you *know* you were called to do to take a back seat. Determine what action you need to take to make that first step.

### *What Are You Willing to Do?*

You need to decide what you are willing to do. Will you make the necessary calls? Will you attend the events to network with your ideal clients? Will you be willing to go outside of your comfort zone? Will you join that program that you know will propel your business? You need to decide if you want to stay where you are, or if you really want to grow your business.

## Kimberly Pitts' Top Business Management Tip

There is a great saying that goes, "What you don't track does not grow." I share with my clients: if you want to grow a sustainable and profitable business, you must track what your business is doing. Sounds simple, however so many entrepreneurs do not spend enough time tracking the activity they do on a daily, weekly, or monthly basis.

As a business owner, you need to know all the numbers in your business such as:

- ≷ How many clients do you have in each program or in general?

- ≷ How many referrals are coming in each month?

- ≷ How many products have you sold?

- ≷ How many people are visiting your website?

- ≷ How many chargebacks or returns did you have?

- ≷ How many customer leads are converting to clients?

- ≷ What expenses are going out each month?

- ≷ How much income is coming in daily?

- ≷ How many new newsletter sign-ups do you have each month?

- ≷ How many people are actually opening your newsletter?

- ≷ How much is your social media reach growing daily, weekly, and monthly?

Taking the time to really understand what your business numbers are saying will:

- ⋧ Assist you to determine which marketing campaigns will work best and when

- ⋧ Help you estimate where to best place your marketing information

- ⋧ Help you determine which Google Ads Words work best at reaching your ideal clients

- ⋧ Help you determine which Facebook posts generate the best results

- ⋧ Assist you in determining which content your subscribers responded to best

So the main question is, "*how* do you track this information?" Simply put, whether you work best with spreadsheets and/or accounting software, find or develop a system where, by the end of each day and month, you are reviewing the items I outlined for you.

If you want your business income to grow, then track the activities of your business.

## Kimberly Pitts' Top Visibility Tip

One thing I would share with any entrepreneur, is that before you create a visibility or marketing strategy plan, you must spend time developing your brand positioning strategy first.

Here is a common scenario. You have a great concept, you develop amazing marketing materials, and you pick the marketing vehicles to launch your concept. Then you start marketing, but you don't generate the type of results you hoped you would.

This typically happens when you don't spend the time to create a brand that your ideal clients are drawn to or feel connected with in some way. The more connected your market is to your business brand, the easier your marketing will be.

When determining how you want to position your business, there are three key areas to branding you must consider. The three components to branding are visual based branding, verbal/communication branding, and behavioral branding. Let's briefly look at behavioral branding.

Behavioral branding focuses on your level of connection to your potential and ideal clients. Some things that you would focus on would be the attributes of your brand, how you are establishing who you are to your market, how you are communicating your value, and how you are connecting to your market.

For example, let's say you state that you are a heart-based, passionate, relationship expert for married couples, and that you have a passion for seeing married couples stay married. When I go to your website, your blog, your social media outlets, or your YouTube channel, I need to feel that you care about my marriage and that you are passionate about saving marriages. If I don't sense that you are as passionate as you stated, then I would keep searching for someone else to work with.

*Quick Branding Assignment:*

You have several entry points into your business, whereby someone can enter. So your brand attributes need to be consistent across the board. Look at all the entry points into your business to see if you are communicating the attributes of your brand consistently.

## Kimberly Pitts' Top Sales Tip

In the world of branding and marketing, your first impression—your headline—can lead to either sales success, or failure.

It's important to realize that headlines work best when they appeal to your reader's interests (not yours). And not only can they *grab attention*, they can also make your message easy to read, convey your main selling points, and lead your customer to a sale.

Here are my favorite types of headlines to use:

1.  The Question

"Are You Bothered About Your Financial Future?"

A question headline works to automatically get your readers involved in your message, because they answer it in their minds. Many people will continue to read further into your marketing materials just to find out what answer or solution you provide.

2.  The How-to

"How to Attract 10 Clients in 10 Days."

How-to headlines work very well, because people love information that shows them how to do something. Think of the benefits your product/service offers and then try creating some "how to" headlines.

3. The Testimonial

"Crystal Jackson's Boot Camp Was Life Changing—I Lost 15 Pounds in 30 days . . . The Right Way!"

Why not let your clients do the selling for you? Their testimonials can go a long way in convincing others to use your services. Tip: To appear credible, always include your clients' full names and the cities they live in.

4. The Command

"Boost Your Productivity by 50 Percent Today!"

Turn your most important benefit into a commanding headline, such as "Make More Time for Your Family," "Look Younger Instantly!" and "Get 7 New Clients This Month." (By the way, throwing a number into your headline is another good tactic. Here's a *bonus tip*: readers seem to like odd numbers as opposed to even numbers.)

5. The News

"Introducing Our New 'Done For You' Services!"

Use this headline only if you truly have something to announce that is of interest to the market.

## Kimberly Pitts' Top Money Tip

The phrase *"Law of Attraction"* gets thrown around often. However, it is real and it does affect us every single day. You attract what you put out there in the world.

Let me show you how this relates to money. I want you to look at how revenue comes into your business and how your clients pay you. You are in business to make a profit. Therefore your relationship with money has to be in tact if you want to be successful.

You may have experienced people not paying you as promised, being late on payments, bouncing checks, or clients needing to make special payment arrangements.

Are you attracting this to your business? Here are some important questions to ask yourself:

> ≥ Are you often late on your bills?

> ≥ Do you find yourself calling your vendors, creditors, and anyone you owe, asking them to move your payments until later?

> ≥ Do you tend to second-guess purchases you make?

> ≥ Do you buy items and habitually return them to the store?

> ≥ Do you make promises to pay, and when you can't, do you contact that person to let them know?

> ≥ Do you research your buying decisions for weeks and months?

Now, think about how your clients handle money with you:

> Do your clients back out of contracts?

> Does it take them forever to make a decision to buy your services?

> Do their credit cards decline?

> Are they always asking for special payment plans?

> Are they unwilling to invest at high amounts with you?

Do you see the correlation between how your clients treat you and how you deal with your personal finances? How you handle money in general will be reflective of how your clients treat you when it comes to payments and working with you.

**About Kimberly Pitts**

Kimberly Pitts is a Marketing and Branding Strategist who provides coaching and business implementation/strategy programs for women entrepreneurs. She outlines how to establish your brand positioning, develop effective marketing plans, create systems for your business, attract and retain your ideal clients, and strategically build your business for maximum results.

**Learn more about Kimberly Pitts at UImpact.net**

# Chapter 19

# ≷Brilliant Tips≷ from Lisa Rehurek

I am so thrilled to share with you my tips for business success. As entrepreneurs, we are a family; we need each other. We need to have like-minded people around us to share our wins, our successes, our failures, and our challenges. I'd also say we are a giving bunch, us entrepreneurs. We *want* to help others. We want to prevent others from having to hit the same roadblocks that we've run into.

This chapter is dedicated to all of you hard-working entrepreneurs who are committed to plowing through, to chasing your dream, and to never giving up. I share with you my favorite learning experiences, my top tips in these five key areas, in hopes that you will be able to avoid some of the same pitfalls that I've run into. I know that there were so many other pitfalls I was able to avoid because of the mentors I've had in my life. I'm proud to be able to pay it forward. I celebrate you and your journey!

## Lisa Rehurek's Top Mindset Tip

### *Get Selfish With It!*

The biggest mindset tip I can give you is just to be true to who you are. Sounds cliché, I know, but here's the deal: when we constantly fight against who we truly are at our core, we screw ourselves up. That's when we really run into confidence issues, and we start comparing ourselves to other people. It's a downward spiral and it can really trip you up.

If you can get in touch with who you are, and really know what *you* want—not what the people around you want, but what *you* truly want—then your mindset stays in a much better place. When you know who *you* are, there is no competition. It's a win-win all the way around.

"But Lisa, that's so selfish!" Look, I'm not telling you to not give to, share with, and nurture those around you, but if your bucket is full, then you have so much more water to give to everyone else. Take care of you first and foremost. We have to stop living our lives based on someone else's dream; that never, ever pans out. It's okay to be focused on what you want, I promise.

I'm going to give you a second tip. Starting and running a business can be hard, it can be trying. Surround yourself with positive people, so you can stay positive. That means weeding out the negativity, which can be hard. You don't have to do it overnight, but avoid those people as much as possible. Play with like-minded people—the big thinkers, the go-getters—who will push you to play your biggest game, and support you as you step into your greatness.

## Lisa Rehurek's Top Business Management Tip

### *The Ugly Truth: Plan*

Ideas start businesses. Action and implementation grow businesses.

As entrepreneurs, we spend so much time dreaming, visioning, and being excited about the bigness of our mission. That's what makes us entrepreneurs. Yet we also want to see results, and all of that dreaming isn't going to do you any good if you don't make progress. You have to have a plan, that's all there is to it. If I were to tell you that you can reach success faster with less heartache and pain, would that peak your interest?

Let me share with you a way to get started. First, identify your 12-month priorities; you will want to identify between three and five. Think about what will make you happy at the end of 12 months. What accomplishments will define success for you? Write them down. Second, in each of those areas, identify where you are now. Please be honest, that's actually what trips people up the most. Be super honest, even if it's painful. Where are you now? Third, look at the gap between where you are now, and where you want to be, and identify specific, actionable tasks that need to take place to get where you want to be in 12 months. This exercise does several things for you:

1.   It helps you identify whether or not your priorities are reasonable within that 12 month timeframe.

2.   It shows you what needs to get done, and provides you with your action plan for the year.

3.   It provides milestones to keep you on track.

Every day, you should be making forward progress toward your goals, even if it's itty bitty baby steps. Course-correct where necessary, but stay the course and you will be popping the champagne at the end of the year to celebrate your amazing successes!

## Lisa Rehurek's Top Visibility Tip

### *Don't Skimp, Invest!*

There are so many different pieces of your business that fall into the "visibility" category. I can speak from personal experience, and also from watching so many entrepreneurs around me, that this is one place where you should invest the appropriate time and money to get the right messages into the marketplace.

If you think about all we have to deal with here—social media, differentiators, the ideal client, branding, marketing messages, public relations, marketing strategy—the list goes on, and it's exhausting! It's easy to get lost.

There are two main categories that I suggest investing time and money in: advice and connection.

### *Advice*

Get some help. I'm here to tell you, you can't drink the wine if you're drowning in the glass.

There are a lot of people out there who specialize in marketing, some are broad and others are very niched. It can be overwhelming. Develop a strategy, do your homework, ask for referrals from others whose marketing resonates with you, and don't be cheap. Get the right person or people who can help you see what you can't see.

### *Connection*

Investment goes beyond just hiring a marketing specialist. There are other ways to invest that fall into the "pay to play'" category. Whether it's writing a book, joining a high level mastermind, getting involved with a specialized networking group, or connecting with media contacts, sometimes you have to pay to play. Don't jump at everything, but pick a few select opportunities, assess them based on your business needs, and jump in where appropriate. It will move you forward at a more rapid pace, like it or not.

## Lisa Rehurek's Top Sales Tip

### *Embrace, Love, and Hug Sales with All Your Might*

I have just two words for you: do it! That's literally my top tip; I could be done writing with just those two words.

If you hate sales, if you're uncomfortable with the topic, it won't go away. Don't procrastinate, don't shy away. Jump in and do it, and get used to it. You can certainly delegate your sales, but in the early stages of your business, you just have to get in there and do it. Practice, practice, practice so that you can *love* it. If you embrace sales, everything else will come so much easier.

Develop a weekly plan for your sales calls, whatever those look like for you. Create focus hours to do nothing but sales, and don't allow yourself to get distracted. And never, ever let a connection go without solid follow-up.

I want to add that you'll see a theme throughout my chapter, and that is: *be you!* It's essential in all aspects of your business, including sales. You will learn a lot of tactics (which I love, of course), and you will gain a lot of knowledge around different processes, but if you don't do what feels right to *you*, it won't work. We try to fit things into the box that someone else has had success with. Take that and learn from it, yes; but use the pieces that feel authentic to who you are, and don't worry about it being the exact same process. It worked for that person because that fit who they are. For strong and sustainable sales results, let it come from the genuine you.

## Lisa Rehurek's Top Money Tip

### *Know Your Numbers*

Even this tip title is boring, I know. I'll be honest, this is my least favorite topic, I am not a number-loving gal, but what does get me jazzed is that when I know my numbers, everything in my business runs much more effectively. If you're like me and not exactly jumping for joy at this topic, here's a little game you can play with yourself: figure out what you want to spend money on that will be motivating to you, and then tie it to the numbers. That will give you a level of excitement to get this piece done. For me in my business, it's almost always getting more help. I can see clearly what I need to do to make that happen, all because I know my metrics.

I'm not just talking about knowing your revenue and expenses, or your profit and loss. Those are certainly important, but there are other key metrics that will help you hire better, outsource more effectively, invest more wisely, and keep more money. Intrigued?

So what kind of metrics should you know, you ask? Here are my top five recommended metrics that will help you make better decisions in your business:

1. How much does it cost to obtain one lead?

2. How many leads does it take to make a sale?

3. How much does it cost to acquire one customer?

4. What is your profit per client?

5. What are your profit and productivity margins for each product or service?

Knowing these metrics, you can better predict the future. You'll know the time and money investment needed to make one sale. You'll know where your time is best spent. You'll know when it's time to bring in extra help. The list goes on. It sets you up to be a real business owner, like the big boys (and girls).

**About Lisa Rehurek**

Lisa Rehurek is an entrepreneur, a dog lover, a fun-seeker, a bit of a party girl . . . oh, and a strategic action mentor, speaker, and international best-selling author. She's obsessed with learning business, studying the latest and greatest, and discovering new innovations. Lisa brings that obsession to each of her clients, sharing knowledge along with a lifetime of business experience. She helps her clients create simple and efficient steps and processes for forward action and crazy good results. Lisa says, "Be Brave. Be Bold. Be You in Business."

**Learn more about Lisa Rehurek at BraveInBusiness.com**

# Chapter 20

# ƸBrilliant TipsƷ from Tracy Repchuk

**Tracy Repchuk's Top Mindset Tip**

As an entrepreneur with over 30 years experience, there are definitely some mindset practices that have kept me going through everything that can hit a business.

I'm going to give you a few that I follow, because if I gave you just one, it wouldn't cover all on which I operate.

Here are my top mindset tips for success:

1.  Create a dream board and put your vision on it. Visuals are great for driving you forward and keeping you motivated. You can add the practical parts once you know where you're going.

2.  Know that nobody can take your dreams. Only you can walk away from them, give them up, let them be taken, or let them die.

The bottom line is you can be your own worst enemy. You're the only one who can make it work or not.

I remember when I started my software company with my college boyfriend at the age of 19. After getting engaged and finding out two weeks before the wedding that he was calling it off, and was with someone else, my dreams were shattered. Everything I thought would happen in the land of happily ever after, crumbled. I had a choice then—to let him steal my dreams from under me, or to keep going, so even with a broken heart and an emptied bank account (he locked me out of my own business, and with two mortgages to pay), I took out a loan and bought him out. Nobody was stealing my dreams.

There were a lot of ways that situation could have turned out, but within a year I had turned the business back into a million-dollar company from $200,000 in debt. Your dreams are the fuel to success.

## Tracy Repchuk's Top Business Management Tip

It's so interesting to look at "Business Management" given my history. Over the years, my response to this prompt would have been different had I considered the tools. Right now it's an autoresponder to automate all communications. Prior to that it was computers (they were $20,000 each when I started my business, and we had contact management for sales follow-up, and faxing for invoice distribution)! But to keep this evergreen, I'm going to talk about productivity, because that has been the same.

Our productivity is measured in results. In our business, we use weekly income—target versus actual. We operate on the prioritization of activities that first focuses on sales, client service, and leads, and then systems and structures. Within that, we now have social media as a form of lead generation and relationship building.

Document your progress. That will give you the power to hand it off, outsource, and systemize.

Follow a procedure to facilitate growth and financial security for your company.

## Tracy Repchuk's Top Visibility Tip

There are so many ways to market your business. As you can imagine, because I am in Internet marketing and social media, those are my marketing preferences. However, I look at the Internet as a medium, not the message. I get the majority of my visibility from the stage.

When I started as an Internet marketer, I made over $100,000 in my first five months, and I won *New Internet Marketing Success of the Year.* For this, they flew me—all expenses paid—to Singapore to appear in front of 3400 people for my first speaking engagement. Before that, speaking was never on my radar, but now it is something I highly recommend.

It takes skill to get speaking gigs. I lucked into the industry because I had the natural ability to sell and engage. I got booked immediately and have now spoken in over 35 countries around the world, and made millions of dollars. However, I also invested over $75,000 in educational programs to gain various speaking skills, such as presentation creation, stage presence, closing techniques, irresistible offers, and more. If you're willing to invest in the skill upgrades, then you can make it happen.

So how do you get the gigs once you have the skills? Attend the shows you want to speak at, familiarize yourself with the host, join an organization if they have your audience, and build a relationship. The other way is to get referrals and recommendations from friends who speak. Remember though, that they will need to see you speak first, because their reputation is on the line if you don't sell or engage an audience (depending on whether it is platform or keynote speaking). Lastly, I use LinkedIn. Have your profile and your websites ready to make you look like a professional speaker.

And if speaking in public is not your thing, then use those skills for webinars and teleseminars. It's the same formula for the presentation, and you can sit at home in your pajamas and build your business!

## Tracy Repchuk's Top Sales Tip

Whether you are a natural born seller, or someone who has learned to love it, the bottom line is that every business owner needs it. You can have the greatest company, product or service on Earth, and without sales it remains hidden to the world.

This was something I had to realize the hard way when I was developing  software in the 1980s, and all of us were tech heads. Nobody was selling. So I had to step out of the programming world and put on the sales hat. It was a long, hard route of trial and error. Now there are fantastic training tools, many of which I still buy because sales is a skill worth its weight in gold.

We use every tool we can—the landing page, autoresponders, a complex sales funnel, webinars, teleseminars, stage, and anything in between. The one that I think is a game-changer (in that once it is mastered, you will never go hungry), is the phone—a live interaction—the lost art of true communication! You can do a free strategy call, and upsell from that. You can call and follow up on networking leads. You can even call old clients and see what else they need.

Whenever our sales aren't up to expectations for the month, it's time for "old school." The phone gets picked up. The first thing I tell my clients when they invest in my website creation services is, "Let's put your coaching package together, and then you can get on the phone and sell it until your sites are ready." That's how you make the money you need for stuff you want.

## Tracy Repchuk's Top Money Tip

This is a very subjective topic, in that I don't necessarily follow rules that a financial advisor would provide you. One thing I know about money is that it is an energy. If you keep it flowing, in and out, it's a river that keeps replenishing itself. So I invest in my company or in myself—sometimes as fast as I make it—because it comes back to me many times over.

If there is something you are putting off getting for you or your company, such as training, it directly relates to you achieving the next step. You might want to consider keeping the river flowing. When you halt the progress of your business, you build a stagnant, still pond.

As far as practical tips are concerned, put ten percent of everything you make into a savings account for business viability—and only use it for growth items such as expansion, equipment, and training. That way you never hold your company back in times of slow cash flow.

For going against the grain—I don't pay myself first, and what I love about what I do here is that I make sure I sell enough to cover expenses, obligations, debt, and me. Maybe some months are less for me than others, and if that's the case I know I need to sell more the next month. It's not that I don't feel worthy of getting paid, because I definitely work hard, but to keep a company viable I don't skim off the top and put me first. If my company can't afford to pay me continuously over time, it's a clear indication that I don't have a company—I am buying myself a job. When you work it this way, you can quickly discover whether or not what you are doing is working, and not live under the illusion of building a business.

## About Tracy Repchuk

Tracy Repchuk is an International Bestselling Author, Online Marketing and Social Media Strategist, and speaker. As an award-winning entrepreneur since the age of 19, with over 30 years of business, Internet, SEO, and marketing background, she has helped thousands of clients get their message online fast and effectively. In addition, she has appeared as a technology specialist in National TV segments with ABC7, San Diego Living, Good Morning New Mexico, CNBC, 4 your money, Report on Business, HGTV, FOX, ABC, NBC, KMIR, Daytime, Fox 5 Las Vegas, New Mexico Style, Vegas Inc, The CW, USA Today, Forbes, MSN Money, King5, CW, and over 50 publications, newspapers, and magazines, plus two motivational movies and hundreds of speaking appearances in over 35 countries.

**Learn more about Tracy Repchuk at MarketingSolutionsforBusiness.com**

# Chapter 21

## ≥Brilliant Tips≲ from Carrie Sharpshair

### Carrie Sharpshair's Top Mindset Tip

#### *Three Essential Elements of a Success Mindset*

If you could automatically make decisions and act in a way that gives you a higher likelihood of success, would you want that? I'm betting yes!

Many elements go into the development of a success mindset; here are my three favorites:

1. P-L-A-N

These are the four little letters that make or break your business! You've no doubt heard the saying "Failure to plan is planning to fail." A plan keeps you focused on what needs to be done, reducing distractions that cost you valuable time, money, and energy.

Start with the end in mind. What's the result you're looking to achieve? Why is it important? Then "chunk up" the steps you need to take to get you there.

2. Act

*Thinking* about growing your business is one aspect of a success mindset; however, thinking won't do you any good unless you are *doing* what you've planned.

Examine how you're spending your time. What are you doing? What are your results? What's going on that's preventing you from taking action on your plans? How is that affecting your bottom line?

3.  Profit

Speaking of the bottom line . . . do you know what yours is? Too many service-based business owners are allergic to their numbers. It's an epidemic! The cure is easy: know your numbers!

Profit allows you to pay yourself more, invest more into your business, and enjoy more of what life has to offer. Isn't that why you went into business in the first place?

When it comes to being your own boss, establishing and fine-tuning your success mindset on a daily basis will lead you toward achieving the success you desire. Remember: Plan, Act, and Profit!

## Carrie Sharpshair's Top Business Management Tip

### *Five Keys to Smooth Operations*

I believe there are five specific aspects to great business management. Mastering these will help you run your business brilliantly:

1.  Know your "Why"

Why are you in business? Why are you in the business you are in? It's possible you haven't found that big, burning purpose in life—that's O.K.—just know that having a "why" helps keep you motivated when times are tough.

2. Identify what success means to *you*

It's your business—no one else's, so make sure you're setting yourself up for what you feel is successful.

Take a look at both your personal and professional life. What do you feel the tangible results of your success should be? Also consider the intangibles—how do you want to feel, both personally and professionally?

3. Know how to plan *and* take action

Outline a "top three" list of objectives you want to accomplish. Determine the best strategies to get you there, and get into action!

4. Be an excellent project manager

Your business consists of a series of intermingled projects. Get really clear on the purpose for each one. What needs to be done (scope)? What's the timeframe for completing it (schedule)? What people, tools, and finances are needed (resources)?

5. Work with the best crew possible

Whether you outsource or hire employees, it's vital to find the best people to represent you and your business. Make sure to spend the time to prepare for them and remember to help them help you!

## Carrie Sharpshair's Top Visibility Tip

### Networking, Referrals, and Follow-up

Marketing can be a huge black hole for many business owners. What strategies and activities are right for you? The answer depends on the type of business you're running and how your customers are looking for you.

At the heart of any great marketing plan is your ability to network, build referral partnerships, and follow-up.

Networking is all about getting out there and making connections, both for and with others. There are networking opportunities all around you. Have a plan before heading out, and remember to do more listening than talking!

### Networking Tip

Take notes on the business cards of people you meet. The date, event name or location, and a brief connection point will help you when it comes time to follow up.

Building referral partnerships is another fantastic way to increase your visibility. When you do this, others are talking about and promoting you, your products, and your services. The key here is to know who has access to your ideal clients and how you can help them to refer you.

### Referral Building Tip

Create an introductory letter (or e-mail/phone script) that your partner can use to introduce you.

Remember, no amount of networking or referral building will pay off unless you have a great system for following up. When you are contacting people directly (through phone calls, e-mail, regular mail, etc.) is when you have the best chances for success.

### Follow-up Tip

Develop a checklist for all your follow-up activities in order to stay on track and ensure people don't fall through the cracks.

Last, but not least, be patient! Marketing efforts can take time to pay off. Be consistent and track your results, so you know what's working for you.

## Carrie Sharpshair's Top Sales Tip

### You've Got to Ask!

Does the word "sales" cause your heart to race and your palms to sweat? You're definitely not alone. The idea of "selling" freaks out many service-based business owners. It doesn't have to though.

For you to do the work you love requires you to develop a solid sales process. At the heart of that process is asking people if they want to take the next step with you.

You can figure out just how many people you have to ask by creating your own personal profit formula:

1. Identify your revenue goal.

2. Based on your services and products, determine how many total clients you need in order to reach that revenue goal.

3. Determine your conversion rate (what percentage of "asks" turn into a sale?)

4. Take the number of clients needed and divide by your conversion rate to find out how many people you need to ask to take that next step with you.

5. Now determine in how many days you'd like to reach your goal.

6. Divide the number of people to ask by the number of days to reach your goal to determine how many people per day you need to ask.

Once you know this number, you can put your marketing and sales plans in place to reach your goals.

### *Super Hot Sales Tip*

Plan your sales activities daily and make sure to schedule the time into your calendar. Eliminate all forms of distraction to help you stay focused on the task at hand. Make sure to do the "happy dance" to celebrate each sale!

## Carrie Sharpshair's Top Money Tip

### *Removing Your Emotional Attachment to Money*

Your relationship with money influences every aspect of your business, from valuing and pricing your services to making decisions on investments and growth. Having a healthy relationship with money along with a commitment to being fiscally responsible helps to ensure you will build a sustainable business and prosper financially.

Whether your money "story" is positive or negative you may have an emotional attachment to money that prevents you from taking your business to the next level. Here are a few tips to help you break free from the emotional attachment:

1. Get real about your money "story"—examine the messages you heard about money growing up and how that has shaped you (positively and negatively).

2. Examine your current financial situation. Look at it completely objectively and recognize that the information on the page is just numbers and isn't a direct reflection of you as a person.

3. Identify where your money decisions are holding you back from achieving the level of success you desire.

4. Identify where your money decisions are serving you well.

5. Enlist the guidance of financial advisors (like your accountant) to ensure your business is operating in a fiscally responsible manner.

6. Get help to bust through any limiting beliefs you have or to re-frame an old money story to create a new one.

Removing the emotional attachment to money will allow you to more freely make financial decisions that are in the best interests of your long-term business health.

## About Carrie Sharpshair

Recognized as the facilitator of "aha" moments, Carrie Sharpshair is a master in helping business owners develop the managerial muscles needed to get focused, get clients, and get paid.

She's known as "The Sharp Cookie", because of her ability to cut through the confusion and build a business that works. Get ready to be inspired and motivated to take decisive action and stake your claim as a confident, profitable business owner, now!

**Learn more about Carrie Sharpshair at SimplyStrategicSuccess.com/essentials**

# Chapter 22

# ≷Brilliant Tips≷ from Shari Strong

## Shari Strong's Top Mindset Tip

Mindset. It's a powerful word. Mindset is everything! I believe one of the reasons most businesses fail in the first year is that business owners fail to get into the proper mindset that could take them through a whole year.

Entrepreneurs are usually driven, overachieving, positive-thinking, passionate, and I could go on. However, they need to be able to see a year down the road and know that there are going to be days that are tough.

They may jump in, truly believing they have "gold." They may know they have a viable business product, plan, or service (often that is what gives them the courage to do it). That is the first step.

The next step is to really think about the time it takes to create a relationship with their future customers, fan base, or community. If you build it, they will come . . . but it takes time.

This is where emotional awareness becomes key: being able to look yourself in the mirror and ask these questions:

1.  When I get stressed, how do I react?

2.  In the past, when my plans didn't work out, how did I feel? Did I become angry at others? Did I get stuck? If you did get stuck, how long did it take to get going again?

3. How do I react emotionally, when I am in a financially strapped situation?

It's not the "doing it" that is the hardest part of business; defining who you truly are and being honest with yourself is the hardest part of creating and adopting an entrepreneurial mindset. It will, however, allow you to achieve more in the long run.

## Shari Strong's Top Business Management Tip

Business management is so broad. What that means to you and what that means to me can be two completely different things.

In my experience, business owners, leaders, and managers tend to complicate things. Brilliance isn't in how complicated something is. Brilliance is when you can take something complicated and see the simplicity in it.

### *Make it Simple!*

I just visited a parts manufacturing company that is half American owned and half Japanese owned. These parts include small screws, bolts, fans, pans, etc. One group of employees is responsible to separate the parts and put them in their specific bin.

They started with serial numbers which were placed on each bin. They would match them up. Being human though, the employees would get in a hurry, miss a number, and put a part in the wrong bin.

To make it simple, they use pictures, the exact size of the part. They post the picture on the bin, with the first three numbers of the serial number, and . . . they added another picture. Of what? Animals, a tree, a stop sign, and other things that are easy to recognize and remember.

So each part has its own associate picture, so to speak. Now, the employees remember that screw 123 is a bear. You may be thinking, "Wow!" Their production from those employees has gone up, the misplaced parts have gone down dramatically, and the employees are happier.

So, if you find yourself saying "This is complicated" with any part of your business, ask yourself the question, "What would be the most simple way to do this, say this, or teach this?"

**Shari Strong's Top Visibility Tip**

Once you have your ideal client in mind, the first question is, "Where do they hang out?" Now, I am not going to share about networking, as I am going to assume you have a grasp on the need for that.

An activity that many trainers or experts use is a Lunch-n-Learn model.

What is a Lunch-n-Learn? It is where you take your business to another business, association, or community forum and offer to teach on a subject, for free, over lunch.

What would you teach? If you offer a service, what is the one thing about that service that everyone should know? If you offer a tangible product, what is something useful you could teach people that is related to the product? For example:

Service—*Health and Wellness*

What is the most important thing you think I should know about health and wellness? What could you teach me about that subject, about how to handle it, about how to change my mindset around it?

Create a 30 minute workshop on the above. Do not focus on your service. Focus on adding value to the people at the lunch. At the end of the session, offer to stay and answer questions, and then let them know how to find out more about you. Here is another example:

## Product—*Rocking Chair for Expectant Mothers*

Why would an expectant mother want a rocking chair, other than for decorating a baby's room? What memories can a rocking chair create? Why are you passionate about rocking chairs? Why are you passionate about this group of prospects?

Create a 30 minute workshop on what to expect, and how creating memories, is important.

My point is; whatever the product or service, there is something that can be taught around it. Teach that, from your heart, and your business will grow.

Starting out with Rainbow vacuum sales and encyclopedia sales, then moving on to a direct sales company in the cosmetic industry, to phone sales, car sales, advertising sales, and ultimately selling my services, I have found that sales, is a state of mind.

When we take ownership for the result of the product, and worry if it will work or not, make them money or not, clean their house or not, make them look younger or not, we will have a tough time selling.

If the person selling is confident their product will work, they usually have no problem talking about it. It's when we add a cost or price to the conversation that it changes. Why? You don't like asking for money?

I don't believe it has to do with assertiveness, people, lack of confidence, your relationship with money, etc. It is this: at the very moment a cost or investment is attached, we consciously or unconsciously wonder, ". . . will this work . . . for them?"

If a product is one dollar, and we know it doesn't work, we will not "sell" that product. It has nothing to do with my value, my communication style, or my personality. We know it doesn't work.

Every decision comes from a place of either love or fear. Love meaning "want to" vs. "have to." When we don't feel comfortable asking for money, that comes from a place of fear: fear that our service or product will not work for them, which could lead to other fears. Fear of not being liked, fear of conflict, fear of . . .

We have nothing to fear. If your product or service works when used, as you describe or promise, what is there to fear: them saying "no," or the questions they may ask?

Once you get over *your* fear of *their* actions, reactions, and results, then stating a dollar amount is just about saying the words.

The investment is $xxx.

The product is $xxx.

It just is!

## Shari Strong's Top Money Tip

Measuring progress, effectiveness, and profits are the three areas that will be needed in any business. Measuring profits can be unnerving if it takes months before money starts to come in. So rather than just measure profits, I focus on gross revenues day to day. Yes, we have to be effective and find new ways to save money and cut costs, but to move forward day to day (coming from a place of abundance) measuring the gross is more important.

On the wall, I have a year at a glance calendar. On the top right hand corner of every month, I write in green marker, the total revenue brought in for that month.

It's easy to get down, to start comparing ourselves to others, to get caught up *in* the business. This green mark is something that I can look at and say,

"I generated xxx amount in February, so I can do it again."

Or

"I brought in $xxx in February, $xxx in March, and $xxx dollars in April. I am doing the right things."

Or

"We didn't have any revenues the first six months, but it started the seventh month. What did I do right, and what could I change so it rolls a little faster?"

Measuring revenues is important, tactically, but using it as a way to "coach" yourself will actually help you in your day-to-day motivation.

## About Shari Strong

Shari Strong is a Speaker, Management Development Consultant, and Small Business Development Expert that ignites a new spark toward leadership and strategies on the

"HOW" of adopting new ideas, adapting to change, and influencing others for an impact that is positive and everlasting. Shari can lead you to a strategy or a plan that is simple and produces results that will take you to the next level of success.

**Learn more about Shari Strong at StrongOrganization.com**

# Chapter 23

## ≩Brilliant Tips≩ from Ha Tran

*Top Five Tips for Peak Productivity*

### Ha Tran's Top Mindset Tip

Your business and the rest of your life are not separate entities. Everything you do has to be in harmony: what you do for a living has to be in line with your goals, your dreams, and your ideals.

For instance, if you want to be a great fashion designer, then the jobs you take as you work toward your goal need to be in that area. You won't take a job in a fish market, but you will work for a seamstress or a pattern maker, even if the pay is less than that of other jobs. You will be developing your skills and gaining understanding of your business area.

You will continue to go to school or apprentice with a fashion designer because you want to learn and develop your skills and find a mentor. So while you are making a living, you are using it to advance your goals and learn the basics of your chosen business.

By working at a job that is moving you toward your goals, even though you are only making a living, your life is in harmony—you are taking steps toward your goal. You will be happier and your life will flow.

This is the key to reach peak productivity—you are always working toward your chosen goal. You don't have to motivate yourself to do drudge work (even when it is) because it is all moving you forward. You are doing what makes your heart sing, what you love and are passionate about, and you will find your motivation is in everything that you do.

## Ha Tran's Top Business Management Tip

### *Use Your SOP (Standard Operating Procedures)*

To manage your business effectively and have peak production, it is essential that you put a set of systems into place. Systems bring predictable, desirable results.

You can develop systems for every aspect of your business. They become your SOP (Standard Operating Procedures) and provide predictable results that save time, eliminating the guessing game of results and profits.

Foremost, you need to be clear about the goal—the intended outcome of your business. Why are you in business, where are you going, and how will you get there? Then you can start to develop the systems that will get you there.

Systems are not just for the actual production of a physical product. They are for areas including administration, marketing, sales, R&D (research and development), product making, etc.

Therefore, you must understand what needs to be done at every level and for each step along the way. First, you have to take the time to develop your procedures. This is time consuming, but the reward is having procedures that save time and money in the long run and produce the results you are aiming for.

With procedural systems in place, when there is a problem, it is much easier to identify and fix. You can focus on the place in one system that is not functioning well, rather than wasting time going through the whole business to find the problem. Problems will always come up, but solutions to them are easier to put into place with systems.

Systems save you time by having a clear set of steps to follow with no guess work about what to do next. They save time because everything is organized, and you are not looking for what needs to be there but isn't, or missing vital steps or items.

Systems bring consistency, organization, and efficiency to your business for peak productivity.

## Ha Tran's Top Visibility Tip

To increase your visibility, you can leverage your presence with social media. Choose one or two areas to focus on, and in which you will excel, in order to maximize productivity.

You must commit yourself to be consistent about what you do. Having a system in place is crucial, and will make for much greater success.

For instance, if you want to have a presence on Twitter, understand how it works and master it. When you have mastered Twitter, you can add other social media, one program at a time.

To market effectively, you must come up with a strategy. Just deciding to post when you feel like it won't work, and you will become frustrated. Therefore, you must make decisions and come up with a system that includes a schedule of postings.

You must be clear about your message, and what your intention is for marketing. Mixed messages waste your time and dilute or totally negate your true message. Be consistent with your message, because you will become known for the types of messages you put out, and you will attract the people who think similarly.

Be consistent with both your format and your message. You may try different ones at first, to find what works best, but once you have found a format and a message that work and resonate with your followers, stick with them. Don't change things up just because somebody else seems to be doing it better, or you want to be different. Consistency is essential for your marketing brand, and results take time.

What research do you need to do for your posts? How much time will the writing take? Will you delegate someone to do one or more of these tasks for you? Again, you need to have your systems in place.

How often and at what times will you post? You can post more efficiently and save time by using a social media management service, such as HootSuite or Shoutlet. A tool like this can pump out posts at different times, while you go about your other business tasks.

Now, you are increasing your visibility and being productive!

**Ha Tran's Top Sales Tip**

Making sales is not a haphazard procedure. Go into the sales process without a plan and a set of procedures, and you are setting yourself up for failure, not success. The key to productivity in sales is to have a good set of procedures and follow them rigorously.

For instance, if you are a roofing contractor, you must have a specific set of procedures that are followed every time a potential customer calls. To begin with, when a customer calls, the administrative assistant has a script that she follows. She then gives the information to the salesperson, who calls the customer and sets up the initial appointment.

When the salesperson gets to the customer, he has a specific set of questions to determine what kind of work is needed and what other issues need to be addressed. He asks for permission to check the roof, asks any additional questions, then sets a time to come back with a quote.

When he comes to give the customer the quote, he gives a presentation of what needs to be done as well as what the options are. He has samples of the materials that will be used for the job. He answers any questions and concerns the customer has and then suggests the best option for the client's needs and desires.

He can then close the sale, getting a signed contract and the initial deposit to secure the job. Then he calls the office to schedule the actual job.

Now this may seem like a lot of steps and a lot of work. How can this be productive?

It is productive because all the steps are carefully laid out in the proper order, and the various problems that can arise have already been accounted for in the procedures. Information both for and from the customer is properly collected and shared, without losing important pieces along the way. A customer's needs are determined in an efficient manner, and work can proceed efficiently as well.

## Ha Tran's Top Money Tip

It is essential in a healthy business to know where your money is coming from and where it is going. Bookkeeping is a tiresome task for many of us, and even worse when there is no procedure in place to ease the process.

Your productivity will go up when you have set procedures for keeping track of all your income and outgo.

When you get a receipt, be sure to make a note, just a word or two, of what it is for. This will save you hours of figuring out what it was for later.

Have a specific place where you put all physical receipts, invoices, etc. They don't belong on your dresser, in your pocket, or at the back of your desk. They are too easily lost or misplaced.

Set up a scheduled time to enter your income and expenses. I cannot emphasize this enough. You can do it daily, weekly, or monthly, depending on the number of transactions you have.

Have a proper system in place for recording this information. You can use an accounting program such as QuickBooks, or you may simply have a folder on your computer with spreadsheets in it. The format doesn't matter as much as the fact that you do it, and it is one you can understand and work with.

It is fine to delegate this task, as long as it gets done consistently and you monitor what is being recorded. This way you know that it has been done properly, and you can pay attention to the numbers.

This system will change over time. You don't have to have a perfect system set up to get started, just do it and adjust it as you go along.

You will be amazed at how much more productive you are when you are not chasing receipts or trying to figure out your bank balance. Remember, having a good system in place will make your productivity skyrocket.


## About Ha Tran

Ha Tran has been helping businesses and individuals succeed with her unwavering commitment to see positive changes, company growth and profitability.

Coming into this diverse American culture, Ha has a deep understanding of the difficulties and benefits of being an immigrant, and she is able to bridge cultural divides in business and social arenas. She helps clients find workable solutions and see challenges in a new light. Ha will help you cultivate a productive and efficient workforce, increase sales and profits, and strengthen your cash flow. She will fully support your company and create a sound, healthy infrastructure.

**Learn more about Ha Tran at HaTranSpeaks.com**

# Chapter 24

## ≳Brilliant Tips≲ from Liz Uram

**Liz Uram's Top Mindset Tip**

Persistence! As an entrepreneur, maintaining a positive mindset is crucial. Without persistence and the ability to persevere when there is no visible light at the end of the tunnel, you cannot withstand the certain ups and downs that come with starting your own business. One minute everything is going better than you could hope for. The next minute all hope is gone and you start to think about giving up. Talk about a roller coaster ride! The good news is that the highs and lows even out over time if you stick with it and keep trying.

I started my coaching business completely from scratch and I had to figure it out as I went along. My transition into entrepreneurship was not a nice, neat extension of my corporate background. There were crazy ups and downs, where I was elated one minute and deflated and ready to quit the next, but I did not give in to those feelings. The type of coaching I ended up doing had little resemblance to what I thought I would be doing when I started my business. I learned from my mistakes, I paid attention to the opportunities that were unfolding in front of me, and I persisted until I got on the right track and started to see results.

As you continue to persist, you will see results too. Maybe not the exact results you were hoping for and maybe not as quickly as you would like, but if you consistently take the right actions you will see results. In fact, forget about taking the "right" actions, you might not know what the "right" actions are. Take the best actions you can with the information you have and keep persisting until you see results!

## Liz Uram's Top Business Management Tip

One of the most common areas entrepreneurs struggle with is time management, and why not? As an entrepreneur you are juggling a lot of balls and hoping you can keep them all up in the air. If you are just starting out and lacking the resources to outsource some of the duties, you are probably wearing all the hats and doing all the work in your business. Plus, you probably have other outside responsibilities and interests to fit in on top of it. This can quickly lead to feelings of overwhelm. No wonder!

First, acknowledge that you are doing a lot. Then, use time blocking to get control of where you spend your time. When you feel overwhelmed, it is easy to waste time without realizing it. This leads to stress and distractions, which can lead you to think you have a time management problem. In reality, what you have is a planning problem. Without a plan you can end up doing a little of this and a little of that without ever completing a task.

You can instantly improve your productivity with time blocking. An easy way to get started is to use a weekly calendar with 30 minute intervals for each day. Use color coding to get a visual of where your time is being spent. For example, you can use green for clients, blue for networking, purple for social media, yellow for follow-up, pink for administration, etc. Start the beginning of each week by blocking off appointments and commitments you already have scheduled. Then fill in the spare time—I promise you will have some—with other tasks you need to complete. Give yourself 30 days to get into the habit of time blocking, and once you do, you will find that you have more time than you thought you did.

## Liz Uram's Top Visibility Tip

As a small business owner or solo-entrepreneur, it is extremely important to make yourself known and to reach as many people as possible. My favorite way to do this is by hosting a teleclass. Teleclasses are an affordable and efficient way to reach a bigger audience than almost any other marketing method. Because of the technology available, you can quickly and easily establish a global following, like I have, by using this technique.

Teleclasses allow you to establish your credibility, become known as an expert, and position yourself as the go-to provider in your industry, because you get to showcase your knowledge. Teleclasses give you the means to break away from the competition and create your own category. The key to getting results from teleclasses is to focus in on a specific topic that addresses something your prospects want. By making teleclasses a consistent part of your overall marketing strategy, you will be able to track which topics are most appealing, and this can help you refine your niche.

One of the best things about teleclasses is that you can get started with little to no cost. There are three components you need in order to implement this method:

1. An invitation/lead capture system

2. A conference call hosting system

3. An e-mail system for follow-up

There are free services available for each of these resources that are perfect to start with. As you grow, you can implement paid services with more capabilities.

The bottom line: the most important thing you can do is to establish your position as the number one expert in your category, and teleclasses are the ideal vehicle for getting the visibility you need.

## Liz Uram's Top Sales Tip

Sales is more about mindset than anything. The reason people are afraid of sales is because of the rejection that comes with it. Let's face it, there is going to be rejection. Not everyone wants or needs what you have to offer. It isn't personal. If you can be okay with that, then you will be fine. If you cannot be okay with that, you are going to have a hard time.

Confidence in what you are selling and the price at which you are selling it is crucial. If you do not believe in your offer and the value you provide, it will show. This is why it is so important to own your position. If you own your position you will be able to price your product and/or service appropriately.

It may seem counter-intuitive, but it is much easier to sell a higher priced product or service that you believe in, than a low-cost option that you do not feel very good about. If you have ever undervalued your offer you know exactly what I mean.

The best way to get more sales is to talk to more people, and ask for the sale. I choose the attitude that there are more than enough clients and "No" is not the end of the world. I only need one at a time. If I talk to someone about my services and they see the value, and want to move forward, great. If I talk to someone and make the offer, and now is not the time, no problem. I review every sales conversation I have, to see what I could do differently the next time, and I try to keep improving with every opportunity.

## Liz Uram's Top Money Tip

Unless you happen to be an overnight success or are already independently wealthy, money is going to be a concern at some point. Protect your profits by making smart decisions when it comes to marketing. Marketing will be your biggest expense for a while because you need to get the word out. However, when it comes to marketing, there are a lot of Bright Shiny Objects (BSO's) out there that can eat up your profits with nothing to show for it except a lower bank balance. BSO's come in many different forms. They can drive you to distraction and convince you that your business cannot possibly thrive or survive without them.

My best tip for avoiding BSO's and saving money on your marketing is to develop a marketing statement. A marketing statement is your stated purpose for every marketing method you implement. In short, it addresses your reason for marketing (to get more leads), how you market (online/in person), and who you market to (ideal client).

Your marketing statement is written while you are in a logical frame of mind and thinking clearly about your business. It acts as a reference point before jumping at every BSO that comes along. Here's an example: a postcard advertisement promises to get your business in front of 10,000 consumers. It is literally bright and shiny. You almost fall for it until you refer back to your marketing statement which states you market online to other businesses. You realize it is not a good fit and you just saved yourself hundreds, even thousands of dollars!

## About Liz Uram

Liz Uram is the owner of The Coach & Mentor Group. She works with business owners to create profitable business models by following her signature six-step business development and planning process.

With over 15 years of corporate and entrepreneurial experience, Liz brings a wealth of relevant and practical information to her clients around the globe. She is an award-winning speaker, the author of several workbooks for entrepreneurs, and a certified professional coach.

**Learn more about Liz Uram at
CoachandMentor.net**

# Chapter 25

# ≩Brilliant Tips≩ from Alicia White

**Alicia White's Top Mindset Tip**

Successful business owners have a take charge and can-do attitude. They have the ability to take a negative and turn it into a positive. They aren't afraid to step outside of their comfort zone and feel discomfort. They also don't hesitate to perform tasks that aren't always fun or exciting. These characteristics stem from a mindset that is willing to overcome challenges, learn, and move forward.

As you build your business, you will be tested and required to step outside of your comfort zone over and over again. Often times, there is extreme discomfort in being tested and taking that step. By being willing to be uncomfortable and enduring temporary discomfort, you can expect growth in your business.

It is hard to be willing to be uncomfortable; no one wants to feel anxious or experience emotional roller coasters in business. Know though, that as you continue to be tested and step outside of your comfort zone, the discomfort lessens until it eventually becomes non-existent.

Instead of avoiding a task that you absolutely despise doing, set aside 15 minutes and perform the task. Feel and acknowledge the discomfort for the entire 15 minutes and then set it aside. Repeat this exercise and extend the duration, and you will find that the discomfort is gone or, at the very least, it has become a comfortable discomfort. Once you change your mindset and set aside your hesitation and avoidance, you can overcome any struggle.

## Alicia White's Top Business Management Tip

No matter how much planning or preparation goes into managing your business, mistakes are bound to happen. Sometimes we forgo obtaining a signed contract to be more flexible with a client, or we advertise a price for a service or product, only to discover later that we undervalued ourselves. It is easy to dwell on the negative impact when this happens. However, this is a great opportunity to learn and improve business practices.

Most leaders will tell you that making mistakes helped them become successful in business. They implemented systems, created checklists, and learned better business practices and management through pitfalls, trials, and failures. No matter the level of education or experience, business owners will inevitably make a mistake. How the mistake is handled is what determines whether or not a business fails or grows.

When a mistake is made, quickly correct the issue. Apologize and accept responsibility; there is nothing wrong with making an honest mistake. People who take responsibility have a greater chance of salvaging a bad situation than those who pass the buck or refuse accountability. It is perfectly acceptable to ask those involved for patience and understanding; after all, they are human and make mistakes, too. Finally, learn from the mistakes made and implement changes to avoid future preventable mistakes.

## Alicia White's Top Visibility Tip

While watching TV, an animation commercial comes on with a plump white polar bear that rolls onto his back and takes a large sip out of a glass bottle held between his paws. No logo is displayed but you instantly know that this is an advertisement for Coca-Cola. In 1993, Coca-Cola adopted the animated polar bear as one of its marketing campaign mascots and it is still as effective and memorable 20 years later.

The reason? Branding.

Plain and simple, if your business is not properly branded, your company will not be visible or memorable. Because it takes seven to ten impressions for an individual to recall a business after seeing an ad or promotion, a stable brand image and effective marketing strategy is crucial. And with new advertising streams becoming more accessible so quickly, it is vital to develop a brand that is consistent, concise, and creative:

- Maintain a consistent brand across all platforms—from websites and social media profiles to business cards and brochures. Display your logo and colors exactly the same way on all of your marketing materials when possible.

- Be concise by developing your message around the problems your clients face and the solutions you provide. Use short, easy to understand words and bullet points to highlight benefits and features.

- Implement creative strategies to deliver your message to keep your brand visible. Create a fun event and ask clients to photograph or record themselves participating, and post the submissions on the company website or social media (always ask permission first).

## Alicia White's Top Sales Tip

Just like many other business owners, I can't stand making sales phone calls. Even if a potential client wanted me to call them, I sat at my desk, staring at the phone, with my gut in knots, and my head swimming with dread. I avoided making phone calls about my business for so long, it affected my profit.

Then my friend, Paulette Ensign, shared with me that I wasn't making sales calls, I was visiting with people I wanted to learn more about and who wanted to learn more about me. She suggested that as they tell me about their needs and desires, I find an opportunity to share with them a service or product that I provide. Now *that* is the type of sales call I can make!

Sales calls are crucial to a successful business: this is how you close the deal. To get to the point of "visiting with people," networking is key. Visit networking groups where the people in attendance are your target audience. Find at least one person who sincerely wants you to call them and discuss your offerings further. Send a follow-up e-mail to schedule a phone visit with them.

If you can't find a group that works for you, try this: attend a meeting without looking for a client. Instead, connect with people who will make a good strategic partner, affiliate, or referral associate. Building relationships with these connections is an excellent way to get introduced to prospects. Once introduced, schedule a phone call visit and learn about your prospect, and then close the deal!

## Alicia White's Top Money Tip

No matter the stage of your business, to grow financially, your pricing must be defined. For business owners who deliver a product, pricing comes easy because profit is based on hard costs. For those offering services, like web design, copy editing, or consulting, defining a price can be tricky. You can quote your hourly rate, but your client needs the total cost of your services to make a budget-driven decision. An hourly rate of $50 sounds like a steal, but if it takes ten hours for you to provide the service, $500 may be more than the client bargained for.

Define your service price by determining the hourly rate for your job title in your industry. There are resources that provide guidance in defining your hourly rate and take into account factors such as your experience, client demographics, overhead, and client geography.

Once you set your hourly rate, list all services you routinely provide. For each service, multiply *your hourly rate* and the *number of hours* it takes to deliver the service to your client. This amount is the total cost you quote to clients. If you don't know how many hours it takes to deliver a service, the next four or five times you perform the service, document each minute you spend and average the number of hours.

For example, copy writer Penny charges $50 an hour. Since it takes Penny three hours on average to write a press release, she quotes clients $150 for one press release. Penny would be doing her clients and business a disservice if she only quoted an hourly rate.

## About Alicia White

As a category creator in the speaking industry and founder of Back of the Room Productions, Alicia White is committed to providing quality marketing design and branding strategy. Having vast experience in print media, graphic design, and content creation, she creates compelling products for speakers, coaches, business experts, and thought leaders whose image demands high-level professional brand presentation.

Alicia is a speaker and author, speaking to business professionals on "The Three Cs of Branding" and "Monetizing Your Message."

**Learn more about Alicia White at BackOfTheRoomProductions.com**

# Conclusion

*Yes*, yes, yes! What was once a mystery to you—the determined entrepreneur—is now clearly revealed, right here within the indispensable pages of this valuable book. Think of it as your business partner!

To expand your ability and reach your potential, it is vitally important to surround yourself with great minds. Although your ideas and actions may seem ingenious to *you*, there are others who may challenge them. The 25 mentors you met here, want to not only challenge you, but see you excel and thrive.

This book holds the answers to your most critical business questions, and presents you with an array of easy-to-grasp strategies, tactics, tips, and tools. Now success is up to you.

If you want to flourish as an entrepreneur, you certainly can. If you're ready to leave your mark on the world, and put a bundle in your bank account, it's time for action. Take what you've learned right here, to make an impact and a profit!

As you move onward into your business endeavors, keep this must-have resource at your desk and close to your fingertips. Reach for it when you need a definite direction or a quick reminder in the areas of mindset, management, visibility, sales, and money. That way, you're certain to break free and succeed.

Every one of the fabulous mentors who wrote in *25 Brilliant Business Mentors-Their Top Tips to Catapult You to Success!* could teach you for days, weeks, and months about how to succeed beyond your wildest expectations. Consider reaching out to any one of them, to be mentored more formally and personally. It could elevate you to glorious new heights.

**Is there a book in you waiting to spring forth?**
*We would love to help you become a published author!*

***Splendor Publishing*** helps entrepreneurs and individuals with important life-work become published authors. Our books encourage personal, professional, and spiritual growth. *Splendor* books are written by experts who want to share their message with the world in a big and brilliant way!

We publish soft cover, hard cover, and digital books for popular readers and devices, in black and white or full color, with professionally designed covers you will be thrilled to present to your peers, clients, friends, and colleagues.

Nothing "reads" credibility and expert status like being a published author. Get better speaking engagements and greater media exposure, too.

Perhaps you're just in the idea stage, or you've begun writing your content. Or, maybe you may have no idea where or how to begin. No worries! *Splendor Publishing* will guide you each and every step of the way, to complete your own book, or even a group book project with two or more co-authors.

Whether you want to compile an anthology of many writers, write your own book to promote your business or ministry, or collaborate on a project for your non-profit or community organization, we can help. Our anthology books are fabulous for marketing, training or fund-raising.

**Let us help you make your dream of being a published author a reality.** Contact Splendor Publishing today at 979-777-2229 or visit **SplendorPublishing.com.**

184

www.ingramcontent.com/pod-product-compliance
Lightning Source LLC
Chambersburg PA
CBHW060547210326
41519CB00014B/3386